DEPARTMENT OF HEALTH AND SOCIAL SECURITY

# The Report of the Committee of Inquiry into the Case of Paul Steven Brown

*Presented to Parliament by the Secretary of State for Social Services*

*by Command of Her Majesty*

*December 1980*

*LONDON*

HER MAJESTY'S STATIONERY OFFICE

£5·30 net

Cmnd 8107

ISBN 0 10 181070 9

## REPORT OF THE COMMITTEE OF INQUIRY INTO THE CASE OF PAUL STEVEN BROWN

MEMBERS OF THE COMMITTEE

| | |
|---|---|
| M Morland Esq QC | (Chairman) |
| Dr P Barbor | Consultant Paediatrician<br>Nottingham University Hospital |
| D Clifton Esq | Director of Social Services<br>Bedfordshire |
| Miss A Salvin | Area Nurse (Child Health)<br>Sheffield Area Health Authority (Teaching) |

*Secretary to the Committee*
Mrs U Brennan

# CONTENTS

Paragraph No

## LIST OF FIGURES

# INTRODUCTION

i. The Secretary of State, in the exercise of the power conferred by Section 98 of the Children Act 1975 and Section 84 of the National Health Service Act 1977 appointed us on the 4th March 1980 as a Committee to inquire into:

a. **What information or professional opinion relating to Paul and Liam Brown existed, was made available to, or could have been obtained by, the relevant authorities;**

b. **The action taken by any relevant authority or by any individual in connection with such information or professional opinion;**

c. **The arrangements for communication within and between the relevant authorities and other persons and agencies holding information about Paul and Liam Brown;**

d. **The working relationships of the Social Services Committee within the Metropolitan Borough Council of the Wirral in so far as they are relevant to the discharge of functions of that Committee in relation to children**

and to report.

ii. On the night of the 11th August 1976, Paul Brown, aged 4 years 3 months, was admitted to Birkenhead Children's Hospital. He was deeply unconscious and in an appallingly neglected state. He had extensive bruising, was highly emaciated and was in a filthy condition. The following day his younger half-brother, Liam, aged 3 years was admitted to the same hospital for investigation. Liam was found to be filthy, verminous and ravenously hungry. On the 19th November 1976 Paul died from his injuries.

iii. From the 17th February 1976 until their admission to hospital the boys had been living at the home of their step-grandparents Stanley and Sarah Brown in Woodchurch, Birkenhead. On the 11th October 1977, at the Liverpool Crown Court, Stanley and Sarah were sentenced to terms of imprisonment for ill-treating and neglecting the boys. In passing sentence Mr Justice Hollings commented that 'It may well be that Stanley and Sarah should not have been allowed to have care of the two boys'.

iv. As a result of this comment the Director of Social Services for Wirral was asked to produce a report which was considered by the Social Services Committee on the 19th October 1977. The concluding sentence of the report read:

> 'Having considered the facts of the case and examined the performance of the personnel involved in its management, I am satisfied that the management and staff did everything that could be expected of them in the circumstances'.

This conclusion did not satisfy the Committee. An inquiry was therefore commissioned, to be held in private before an independent panel under the chairmanship of Mr J Stewart Oakes, a Recorder.

v. The Oakes Inquiry, which lasted 4 days, held its first meeting on the 27th February 1978, and reported on the 28th March 1978. The Oakes report was critical of the Social Services Department and of individuals working within it and made various recommendations on the improvement of services in connection with non-accidental injury to children in the Wirral area. The staff of the Social Services Department were however unhappy at what they regarded as errors of fact in the Oakes report. The Social Services Committee also had grave doubts as to the basis and the findings of the report because of the absence of any reference within it to an apparently material document which some Councillors said they had seen. This document, which has come to be know in the Wirral as the 'missing memo', was said by the Councillors to contain a recommendation that Paul and Liam should not be placed with Stanley and Sarah Brown. Following consultation with the Chairman of the Social Services Committee the Chief Executive selected Mr Price-Jones, Deputy Director of Administration and Legal Services, to conduct an investigation as to the existence or whereabouts of the 'missing memo'. His conclusion was that: 'On the basis of the available evidence one must conclude that the existence of the alleged memorandum cannot be proved'. As a result of Mr Price-Jones' investigations Wirral Borough Council decided to establish a further independent inquiry into the missing document. This second independent inquiry was held on the 25th July 1978 before Mr Mervyn Heald, QC.

vi. The Heald Inquiry was not a statutory inquiry and therefore had no power to compel the attendance of witnesses. This proved to be a severe handicap as the staff of the Council, following the advice of the National and Local Government Officers Association (NALGO), declined to give evidence. Mr Heald therefore heard only one side of the story. In his report dated the 6th October 1978 Mr Heald reached the conclusion that a written report indicating that Stanley and Sarah Brown were unfit to have the care of the boys was in existence in March 1976 and that this report, although seen in the room where the Oakes Inquiry had been sitting on the 1st March 1978, was not shown to the Oakes Committee. He also made reference to 'a skilful amendment' to an entry dated the 26th March 1976 in the running record on the social work case file on Paul and Liam. Thus the Oakes Committee had apparently made a report in ignorance of material documentary evidence.

vii. Mr Heald suggested that the Council might wish to consider making a formal request to the Secretary of State for a statutory inquiry with the power of subpoena for the purpose of enforcing the production of documents and the attendance of witnesses. The Council applied to the Secretary of State on the 13th October 1978 but their request was refused.

viii. Serious public disquiet continued and the case received a great deal of coverage in the media. In particular the Wirral Globe newspaper reported in a series of articles on the campaign by the Mayor of Wirral, Councillor Wells, for a full statutory inquiry to expose what he described as a 'cover-up' involving senior staff of Wirral Social Services Department. On the 30th November 1979 Mr Frank Field, MP for Birkenhead, and Mr David Hunt, MP for Wirral, raised the Paul Brown case on an adjournment debate. During this debate Sir George Young, Parliamentary Secretary (Health), said that he would like to initiate 'a proper inquiry' and would consider what powers were available to the Secretary of State. On the 20th December 1979 Sir George Young announced the intention to establish our Committee of Inquiry.

ix. The terms of reference of our Inquiry were announced publicly in a press release on the 20th February 1980 in which anyone who wished to give evidence was invited to contact the Secretary to the Committee. We opened the Inquiry with a preliminary hearing held in London on the 14th March 1980 at which the procedure to be followed was announced and applications for representation were made.

x. The Inquiry was held in public on 50 days between the 12th May 1980 and the 18th July 1980 at Bebington Civic Centre, Bebington, Wirral. We heard oral evidence from 94 witnesses and received written statements from a further 6 witnesses. We required all witnesses who appeared before us either to take the oath or to affirm. We also considered 262 documentary exhibits amounting to more than 3,300 pages. We visited the 5 Area Offices of the Wirral Social Services Department and the accommodation formerly used by the Birkenhead Area Office. We also visited the Social Services Department headquarters where we were shown the Child Abuse Register (formerly the At Risk Register) and various specialist teams.

xi. We had the assistance of four members of the Treasury Solicitor's Department who, under the leadership of Mr Michael Mead, collected all the relevant documentary evidence for us and took statements from witnesses. We are grateful to Mr Mead and his team for their efficient presentation of the evidence which made our task much easier. The Treasury Solicitor instructed Mr Simon Fawcus and Mr Keith Armitage of counsel to appear on behalf of the Committee and we should like to place on record our appreciation of the assistance which they gave us. The facts were outlined to us in opening by Mr Fawcus and advocates of represented parties made short opening statements. Witnesses were examined-in-chief by their advocate or by counsel to the committee if they were unrepresented. They were cross-examined by each party who wished to do so and, at the end of the cross-examination, re-examination of the witness by the person who had conducted the examination-in-chief was allowed. At the conclusion of the evidence closing speeches were made.

xii. We should like to place on record the great help we have had from all advocates during this very long and complex inquiry. In particular we should like to thank Mr Lynch, who appeared on behalf of a large number of NALGO members of the Social Services Department, and Mr Morgan who represented Wirral Borough Council, for the responsible manner in which they conducted their respective cases.

xiii. We would also like to thank our Secretary, Mrs Ursula Brennan, and Assistant Secretary, Miss Marian Taylor, for the unstinting and extremely capable assistance which they gave us throughout the Inquiry and in the preparation of this report for its printing.

## LIST OF WITNESSES

WIRRAL METROPOLITAN BOROUGH COUNCIL—COUNCILLORS

|  |  |  |
|---|---|---|
| Councillor Harry Deverill | Leader of the Council | From May 1977 to May 1980 |
| Councillor Frank Harding | Chairman of Social Services Chairman | From April 1974 to March 1976 |
| Councillor John P Roberts | Chairman of Social Services Committee | From May 1976 to May 1978 |
| Councillor William E Leigh | Chairman of Social Services Committee | Since May 1978 |
| Councillor Kenneth G Allen | Vice-Chairman Social Services Committee | From 1977 to 1979 |
| | Member of Social Services Committee | From May 1975 to May 1979 |
| Councillor Mrs Kathleen Wood | Member of Social Services Committee | From April 1974 to May 1978 |
| Councillor Ian Walker | Member of Social Services Committee | From May 1976 to May 1978 and since May 1980 |
| Councillor David W Allan | Member of Council | Since 1975 |

WIRRAL METROPOLITAN BOROUGH COUNCIL

|  |  |  |
|---|---|---|
| Mr Ian G Holt | Chief Executive | Since April 1974 |
| Mr Peter J Mills | Director of Administration and Legal Services | Since December 1976 |
| Mr Ian Wood | Director of Finance | Since September 1979 |
| Mr Roger E Shaw | Director of Development | Since April 1974 |
| Mr William C W Hughes | Director of Personnel and Management Services | Since December 1976 |
| Mr Paul N Samuels | Assistant to Chief Executive | Since April 1974 |
| Mr Arthur P Price-Jones | Deputy Director of Administration and Legal Services | Since January 1977 |
| Mr Geoffrey C Betteridge | Principal Solicitor, Department of Administration and Legal Services | Since October 1975 |
| Mr Cyril J Swinburn | Administrative Assistant, Department of Administration and Legal Services | |

WIRRAL SOCIAL SERVICES DEPARTMENT—HEADQUARTERS

|  |  |  |
|---|---|---|
| Mr Douglas Jones | Director | Since April 1974 |
| Mr Robin SeQueira | Deputy Director | Since February 1978 |
| Mr Kenneth McDermott | Assistant Director (Fieldwork) | Since April 1974 |
| Mr James O'Shea | Principal Assistant (Fieldwork) | From May 1975 to April 1980 |
| Mr William Brown | Principal Assistant (Personnel and Training) | Since May 1979 |
| Mrs Juliann Penk | Child Care Specialist | From September 1975 to August 1980 |
| Mr Anthony J Matthews | Senior Officer Special Child Care Team | Since March 1979 |
| Mrs Valerie Burford | Secretary to the Director | Since March 1978 |
| Miss Isobel Bevan | Secretary to Assistant Director (Administration) | |
| Mrs Alma Caley | Assistant to Director's Secretary | |
| Miss Carol S Cassia—(Statement read) | Shorthand Typist | |

| | | |
|---|---|---|
| Miss Sylvia E Cowgill—(Statement read) | Temporary Secretary to Director | |
| Miss Lynda Darlington | Secretary of Mrs Penk | |
| Mrs Aileen Frowe | Secretary | |
| Miss Sandra Limb | Secretary to Deputy Director | |
| Miss Suzanne McLean—(Statement read) | Typing Pool Supervisor | |
| Miss Margaret McNamara | Secretary to Administration Officer | |

WIRRAL SOCIAL SERVICES DEPARTMENT—CENTRAL WIRRAL OFFICE

| | | |
|---|---|---|
| Mr Horace J Surridge | Area Officer | From February 1972 to October 1975 |
| Mr Derek Evans | Area Officer | Since October 1975 |
| Mrs Pamela Winship | Deputy Area Officer | Since May 1975 |
| Mrs Lesley M G Costello | Senior Social Worker | From January 1976 to June 1979 |
| Mr Kenneth Corker | Senior Social Worker | Since March 1975 |
| Mr Alexander E Pickstock | Social Worker | From December 1975 to 1979 |
| Mr Alan Davies—(Statement read) | Social Worker | Since January 1975 |
| Mrs Pauline Rainford | Team Clerk Typist | From April 1974 to 1978 |
| Miss Marilyn Rowe | Administrative Typist | Since 1974 |
| Mrs Joan Singleton | Typist (Team 1) | |

WIRRAL SOCIAL SERVICES DEPARTMENT—BIRKENHEAD OFFICE

| | | |
|---|---|---|
| Mr Anthony J Hotchkiss | Area Officer | From April 1974 to October 1975 |
| Mr Kenneth Wylde | Area Officer | Since October 1975 |
| Mrs Jean E Gurny | Deputy Area Officer | Since October 1975 |
| Mr Ernest F V Housden | Senior Social Worker | Since April 1974 |
| Mr Glyn Ridge | Senior Social Worker | From August 1975 to August 1978 |
| Mrs Mary E Francis | Welfare Assistant (working with the Homelessness Officer) | From 1973 to 1974 |
| Mrs Jennifer M Tiddy | Social Worker | |
| Mrs Jean Huges-Jones | Social Worker | |
| Mrs Heffer (Mrs Van der Meer) | Social Worker | From Summer 1974 to June 1975 |
| Mrs Sonita M Thornton | Social Worker | Since June 1975 |
| Mr Peter Davidson | Social Worker (Home Teacher for the Blind) | Since 1978 |
| Mr John Carlile | Social Worker | Since June 1975 |
| Mr Ralph Dodd | Social Worker | Since October 1975 |
| Ms Pauline Fox | Social Worker | From October 1975 to January 1977 |
| Mrs Beryl Robertson | Social Worker | Since 1975 |
| Mrs Ena Davies | Administrative Assistant | Since April 1974 |
| Mrs Dilys Jones | Clerk/Receptionist | |

WIRRAL SOCIAL SERVICES DEPARTMENT—HOSPITAL SOCIAL WORKERS

| | | |
|---|---|---|
| Mr John Walker | Principal Hospital Social Worker | From 1974 to 1977 |
| Mrs Mary K Doran | Senior Social Worker (Birkenhead Children's Hospital) | From 1975 to June 1977 |
| Mrs Honor M Neal | Social Worker (St Catherine's Hospital) | From June 1973 |

WIRRAL AREA HEALTH AUTHORITY

| | | |
|---|---|---|
| Dr Kevin Vernon Jones | Consultant Paediatrician | Since August 1974 |
| Dr Margaret Black | Senior Clinical Medical Officer (Birkenhead) | Since November 1973 |
| Dr Helen M Brass | Area Specialist in Community Medicine (Child Health) | |
| Miss Barbara H Taylor | Area Nurse, Child Health Local Authority Liaison | From April 1975 to April 1980 |
| Miss Jean Rowlands | Divisional Nursing Officer (Based at Social Services Centre Cleveland Street Birkenhead) | From August 1975 to March 1978 |
| Mrs Dorothy G Riley | Nursing Officer, Health Visiting (Birkenhead) | Since June 1972 |
| Miss Elizabeth M Morgan | Nursing Officer—Wallasey Sector | |
| Mrs Joan Sowery | Nursing Officer—Birkenhead Children's Hospital | Since 1974 |
| Miss Helen Lloyd | Health Visitor (Woodchurch Clinic) | Since September 1972 |
| Miss Eileen Murphy (Statememt read) | Health Visitor (attached to Doctors Owers and Wetherall at Balls Road Clinic) | |
| Mrs Maureen Sayer | Health Visitor | Since September 1974 |
| Mrs Lilian Weston | Health Visitor (in charge of Miriam Place Clinic, Birkenhead) | |

GENERAL MEDICAL PRACTITIONERS

| | |
|---|---|
| Dr Frederick M Owers | Pauline's GP (Birkenhead) |
| Dr Robert H Moore | Pauline's GP (Birkenhead) |
| Dr Vaughan Roberts | Stanley and Sarah Brown's GP (Woodchurch) |

THE FAMILY

| | |
|---|---|
| Mrs Sarah Brown | |
| Mrs Pauline Brown | |
| Mrs Margaret C Streatfield | Pauline's Mother |
| Mrs Cecilia Whelligan | Pauline's Aunt |
| Mrs Eileen Patrick | Pauline's Aunt |

THE FOSTER PARENTS

Mr William Shackleton
Mrs Sheila J Shackleton

OTHERS

| | | |
|---|---|---|
| Mrs Margaret Anders | Neighbour | |
| Mrs Vera N Bowen | Warden, Balls Road Homeless Families Unit | From 1967 to 1974 |
| Mr John H Cullen | Clerk to the Oakes Inquiry | |
| Mr Roderick H Dawson | Solicitor retained by NALGO to represent NALGO members at the Oakes Inquiry | |
| Mr David Gee | Solicitor to the Oakes Inquiry | |
| Mr Richard Hamilton | Probation Officer (Based at Birkenhead) | Since September 1975 |
| Mrs Rosalind M Hampson (Statement read) | Senior Social Worker (Walton Hospital) | |
| Mrs Marie Hill | Clerk/Receptionist Wallasey Area Office of Wirral Social Services Department | |
| Mr David G Jones | Forensic Scientist (Specialising in the examination of documents) | |

OTHERS—*continued*

| | | |
|---|---|---|
| Mrs Shelah E Jones | Supervisor—Cavendish Pre-School Playgroup | Since 1971 |
| Mr David Kirwan | Solicitor (for Stanley and Sarah Brown at Committal Proceedings) | |
| Mr John B Miles | Consultant Neurosurgeon (Walton Hospital) | Since September 1971 |
| Mr Harry Parsonage | Chief Executive—Wirral Family Practitioner Committee | |
| Mr Edward Wilkinson | Public Relations Officer for Woodchurch Residents Association | |

## CHAPTER ONE

# GENERAL OBSERVATIONS

1. Our weeks of inquiry into the functioning of social and other related services in the Wirral and into the circumstances which led to Paul Brown's death have been a lesson to each of us. So much so that we feel that it would be of benefit to the public at large if we set out some of our general conclusions which might otherwise be buried amidst analysis and detail and be unread except by the specialist reader.

2. In some circles the social worker may conjure up a picture of some young person with unconventional views on society or politics intent upon propagating such views. Such a picture is not in accord with reality. **Each of us was struck by the generally high quality of the social workers who gave evidence to us or about whom others spoke.** They came from a wide variety of backgrounds: some entered social work after university or polytechnic, some much later after years of experience in other fields or professions; others started their working life in some clerical capacity and then found their true bent in social work; some became skilled social workers primarily by experience, others by examination. The ages of the staff range from new young recruits with degrees, through women who have brought up a family and have returned to work, to middle aged social workers with a wealth of experience. In our opinion it is of great benefit to a Social Services Department if its staff at all levels have this variety of background. **Too often the social worker only becomes news when something goes wrong; normally the daily caring work goes on unsung and not excessively rewarded.** We were impressed by the dedication of most Wirral social workers, often going well beyond the call of duty in an environment and in working conditions inimical to such dedication.

3. **We cannot emphasise too strongly the value in both monetary and social terms of the social worker and the health visitor.** They provide care and services for young and old, sick and handicapped within the community. Money wisely spent on the provision of dedicated, qualified social workers and health visitors and on ancillary services is money saved on hospitals, the police, the law and prisons, as the case of Paul Brown tragically illustrates. In the three months before his death Paul Brown was the subject of intensive care and specialist treatment in hospital. The Police had to investigate the allegations of child neglect. Criminal prosecutions were pursued in the Magistrates Court and thereafter in the Crown Court before a High Court Judge. Two people ended up in prison. All this occasioned considerable public expenditure. False economies in the social services and other like services can result in vast expense later of a non-productive kind.

4. **The Paul Brown saga unfolded against a background of financial constraints but we are satisfied that these had no direct effect on the handling of Paul and Liam's case. More money could have bought better accommodation, more social workers and more administrative back up. Indirectly it might have provided more time for thoughtful consideration of Paul and Liam's case but on the evidence which we heard it is doubtful if different decisions would have been taken.**

5. **In the years 1974 to 1976 the Wirral Social Services Department was ill-equipped to deal with problems such as arose in the case of Paul Brown and his family.** Mistakes and errors of judgement were made. We are however happy to be able to record how much excellent work the Department did during these years amidst many difficulties.

6. The admission of Paul Brown to hospital rightly called for an inquiry. It is of the utmost importance that such inquiries are searching and objective. If the facts disclose errors or inadequacies these should not be concealed or minimised out of a false sense of loyalty to staff however hard-pressed, nor should they be used to apportion blame or to find a scapegoat. **The aim of such inquiries should be the improvement of services from lessons to be learnt from the past.** Our Inquiry has been the culmination of a series of internal and external inquiries into this case. These earlier inquiries were inhibited for a variety of reasons and this helped to sow the seeds of suspicion. **We hope that our inquiry will be accepted as final. Since August 1976 the Metropolitan Borough of the Wirral and its Social Services Committee, Department and staff have been working in an atmosphere of mistrust, rumour and recrimination. This has seriously affected staff morale, to the detriment of services provided to the community. It is to the credit of the whole Social Services Department that despite the expenditure of time, money and anxiety on inquiry after inquiry the standard of efficiency of the Department has greatly improved since 1976.** We hope that Wirral Borough Council and all its staff, with the lessons to be learnt from the past, will fact the future together with confidence.

7. In our Report the reader will find no villains, no conspiracy and no deliberate cover-up, only the victims of circumstance and human weaknesses. There were indications at times during our Inquiry of a reluctance to divulge the unpalatable but we have no doubt that this was motivated mainly by misplaced loyalty to colleagues. If villains there be they were local government reorganisation[1] which came into effect on the 1st April 1974 and reorganisation of the National Health Service[2] which came into effect on the same date. Reorganisation had a traumatic effect on social work in the Wirral as elsewhere, coming only three years after the implementation of The Local Authority Social Services Act 1970 which put into effect the reforms recommended by the Seebohm Committee[3]. The 1st April 1974 found social workers in the Wirral ill-trained and ill-equipped to face the challenge. They found themselves doing unfamiliar work with new colleagues in strange places from inadequate premises.

8. **The discharge of functions of a Social Services Department in relation to children is not carried out in a vacuum. Effectiveness depends on morale and efficiency within a Department from the Director downward and on the Director's relations with his own Department with other Chief Officers and with the Council as a whole. We consider that the effectiveness of the Wirral Social Services Department has been lessened by a breakdown in those relationships.**

---

[1] Following the Local Government Act 1972.

[2] Following the National Health Service Reorganisation Act 1973.

[3] Report of the Committee on Local Authority and Allied Personal Social Services Cmnd. 3703 HMSO 1970.

9. A major explanation for the errors of judgement at managerial level in the handling of the Paul Brown case was the morale of the Director and senior management during the years 1976, 1977 and 1978. The relationships between the Department of Social Services and those of Finance, and Administration and Legal Services were not those to be expected of servicing and programme Departments. They were of mutual mistrust and misunderstanding. Personalities as much as policies were responsible but the main ingredient was the style of management of the Director of Social Services.

10. Our report does not make any recommendations as to professional practice. In the years since 1976 Wirral Social Services Department have made many improvements in their procedures and a number of child abuse inquiries have drawn attention to most of the problems which beset the case of Paul Brown. At times in our report we have drawn attention to areas where further improvement is required and where lessons can be learnt. Those who are concerned with services for children will learn about the practical impact of well known problems by reading in the narrative how these problems influenced this particular case.

## CHAPTER TWO

# THE ASSESSMENT OF THE EVIDENCE

11. Although we were satisfied that almost every witness giving evidence to us wished to be both frank and truthful all witnesses laboured under inevitable difficulties. Many of the most contentious matters occurred a long time ago, often four or five years ago. That alone could result in some errors of recollection. Since the 12th August 1976 many witnesses have made statements or given evidence on several occasions in connection with the series of earlier internal and external inquiries. There is a tendency for later evidence to be an amalgam of recollection of actual events and previous statements about those events. In the years 1974–1976 many of the social workers who gave evidence before us were inexperienced and working under stress. Over the years they have become more experienced and some have become qualified. Recently acquired knowledge and experience may therefore have influenced the reconstruction of the past.

12. An atmosphere of rumour and recrimination has existed locally and within the elected members and staff of the Wirral Borough Council. It has also been reflected in the media. This may have caused individuals and Departments to adopt postures with regard to criticisms or allegations. Such postures may lead to a defensive attitude on the part of a witness who out of loyalty to colleagues or Department may be reluctant to divulge documents or evidence which might be inconsistent with his own point of view, or may lead to over emphasis, exaggeration or dramatisation. Our task has been eased by the vast number of genuine contemporary documents which have been put before us, ranging from brief and casual diary entries and notes to formal minutes and reports. Thus we have been able to assess the evidence given to us against the contemporary record. This has had to be done with caution because a document although genuinely contemporary may be coloured by its provenance and purpose. For example a staff memorandum calling for action will be drafted in a manner likely to forward that action. **Nevertheless, despite all the evidentiary discrepancies and problems, we are satisfied that our findings of fact on essential matters are correct.**

13. The evidence given orally before us lasted over 9 weeks. The documents placed before us were very voluminous. The discrepancies in the evidence were very many, the contentions of the people involved and the arguments of their advocates disputatious and complex. Our report would be excessively long and tedious to read if we set out all these matters even in summary form. Therefore except in some instances where we have considered it right to set out detailed evidence and contentions **we set out only the more salient facts, as we found them, to illustrate our conclusions.**

## CHAPTER THREE

# THE BACKGROUND TO THE PAUL BROWN CASE

### The Authorities

14. The two Authorities whose staff were mainly involved in the case of Paul and Liam were the Wirral Borough Council, through its Social Services Department, and the Wirral Area Health Authority (AHA). Until July 1979 Wirral AHA was divided into two Districts, North and South. The structure of the Northern District Community Nursing Division (which was responsible for the Health Visiting Service provided to Paul Brown) as at July 1976, is shown in Figure 1. Apart from providing the Health Visiting Service the AHA is also responsible for the NHS hospitals in Wirral; it is not responsible for the General Practitioner service which is run by the Wirral Family Practitioner Committee. The structure of Wirral Social Services Department, as at July 1976, is shown in Figure 2. Since 1976 various new posts have been added.

15. For Social Services purposes the Wirral is divided into five areas (Birkenhead, Central Wirral—sometimes known as Moreton, Bebington, Wallasey and Deeside) each served by an Area Office. An Area Office serves a number of functions:

a. a place where members of the public can call and seek advice or be interviewed by a social worker;

b. the location for Area Office meetings and case conferences;

c. a place for social workers to write reports, keep up their records, receive supervision, exchange information and make telephone calls;

d. a store for clothing, money and occupational therapy equipment; and

e. an office for the clerk/typists and administrators with room for desks and filing cabinets.

16. In charge of each Area Office is an Area Officer. Each Area Office has a number of teams of Social Workers usually but not always organised on a geographical patch basis, each team being headed by a Senior Social Worker. One of these Seniors will be the Deputy Area Officer, acting as a team Senior in the usual way but also deputising for the Area Officer in his absence. We believe that in Area Offices where there is a heavy child care caseload the Deputy Area Officer should be a full-time Deputy. A full-time Deputy could act as a casework consultant, advising Social Workers and Seniors on the management of difficult cases. In busy Area Offices such a consultant role is not possible if the Deputy also has to run his own team. The Senior Social Workers allocate individual cases to the members of their teams so that each Social Worker has his own caseload for which he is responsible. Each Senior Social Worker is responsible for the supervision of the Social Workers in his team. It is the Senior Social Worker's responsibility to allocate new cases and to oversee the handling of cases, giving advice and support to the Social Worker in charge of the case. The structure of the two Area Offices which featured in the Paul Brown case is shown in Figures 3 and 4.

**Figure 1 Wirral Area Health Authority Northern District Community Nursing Division - July 1976**

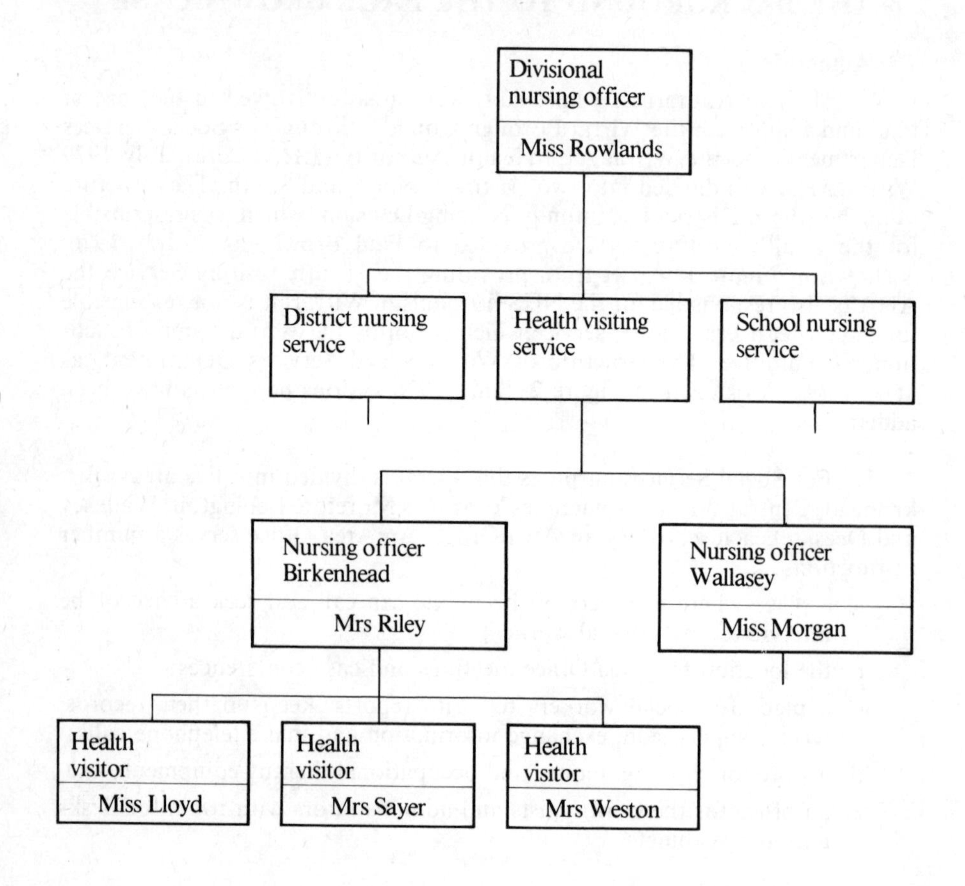

**Figure 2 Wirral Social Services Department 1976**

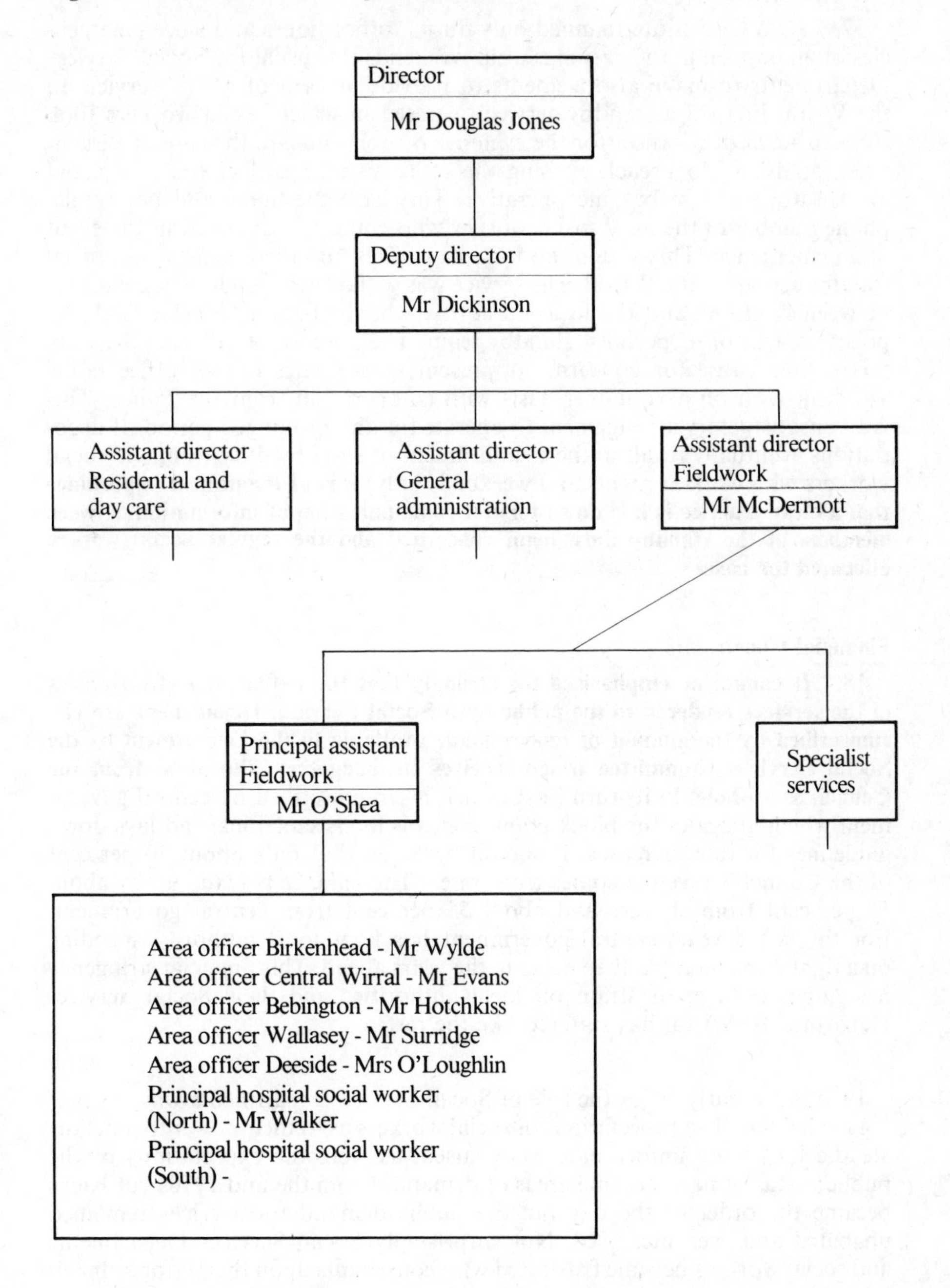

**The Duty Officer System**

17. Area Offices are manned only during office hours and since emergencies often happen in the evenings or at weekends it is usual for Social Services Departments to make arrangements to provide an 'out of hours' service. In the Wirral in 1975 a standby service operated in which social workers took turns to act as duty officer for the evenings or weekends. In the case of Birkenhead, at five o'clock each evening the office switchboard closed down and an Ansafone system became operative. This gave the name and home telephone number of the duty social worker who could be contacted in the event of an emergency. This system no longer operates and there is now no official standby service in the Wirral. The service was withdrawn, pending negotiations between NALGO and the local authority, when it became official NALGO policy to ask for a specialist standby team. The absence of any standby duty service is a cause for concern. At present emergencies out of office hours are dealt with on a volunteer basis with co-operation from the Police. This is an unsatisfactory arrangement to operate for any prolonged period. If negotiations eventually result in the establishment of standby duty teams (ie social workers who work at nights and weekends only) **it is of the utmost importance that a clear practice is laid down for full communication of information between members of the standby duty team concerned and the regular social worker allocated the case.**

**Financial Constraints**

18. **It cannot be emphasised too strongly that the extent and effectiveness of the services rendered to the public by a Social Services Department are circumscribed by the amount of money made available to the Department by the Social Services Committee which receives its budgetary allocation from the Council as a whole.** In its turn the Council is circumscribed by central government which allocates the block grant, controls loans sanctions, and lays down guidelines for rate increases. It should be noted that only about 30 per cent of the Council's revenue comes from rates. The balance is made up by about 15 per cent from charges and about 55 per cent from central government. For the last 5 years central government has kept local authority spending on a tight rein and is likely to do so in the years ahead. This financial stringency has imposed to great strain on local authorities and their Social Services Departments. Wirral has suffered like the rest.

19. In the early 1970s the role of Social Service Departments was expanding in all fields. The expectations of social workers as to their power to ameliorate the lot of the unfortunate were raised, as were the expectations of the public; areas of need became areas of demand. From the mid 1970s cut backs became the order of the day but the public demand for services remained unabated and even increased. Not surprisingly Social Services Departments and social workers became frustrated with constraints upon their efforts. Inevitably friction developed, with on the one hand programme Departments within the local authority all competing for a share in the cake which inflation tended to make smaller each year, and on the other hand the servicing Departments and the Council as a whole trying to adhere to government guidelines and at the same time preserve the quality of services.

**Figure 3 Birkenhead Area Office - July 1976**

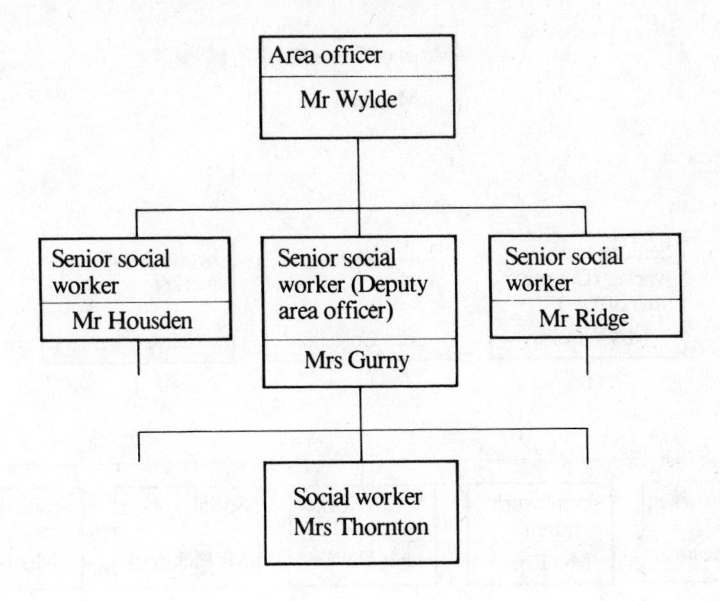

**Figure 4 Central Wirral Area Office - July 1976**

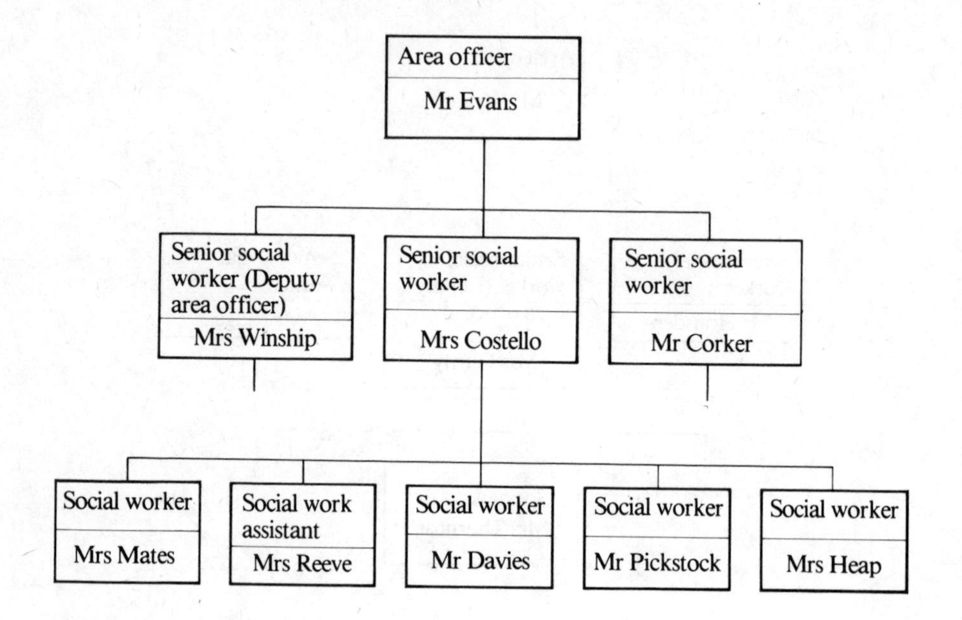

20. The total expenditure available to the Wirral Borough Council, as with other local authorities, is largely determined by government criteria. The Council has to share the available resources among its various Departments. In reality the individual shares are largely pre-empted; each annual budget can make only marginal adjustments between individual Departments. In the Wirral, as in most similar local authorities, Education is the biggest spender, taking 65 per cent of the budget; this leaves a very small residue for allocation between the remaining programme Departments. As the current Director of Finance, Mr Wood, told us:

> 'We just cannot manoeuvre our services sufficiently to swing them about substantially. So we have a firm base for our budget and really it is only the margins that determine from year to year whether there should be a marginal cutback or marginal growth in individual services'.

21. The analysis at Figure 5 shows how the Wirral Social Services Department's share of the budget has increased since 1976/77. **Although on paper this analysis indicates a substantial increase available to the Social Services Department we must emphasise that there will be a significant reduction in real money terms in 1980/81 compared with 1979/80 because of inflation.**

22. Figure 6 shows the effect of government guidelines on Wirral's services and in particular on the Social Services. It should be noted that only in 1979/80 did government guidelines involve growth, and that only of 1·6 per cent.

23. Figure 7 shows the distribution of Social Services expenditure between Residential, Day Care and Other Services.

24. We consider that the public should know in broad outline the financial constraints within which Wirral Borough Council has to work. Only then can the operations of the Social Services Department and the particular parts of its services with which we are concerned be seen in perspective. **Again we must emphasise that the discharge of the functions of the Committee and the Department in relation to children is only a part of its activities. Although we have centred our attention on children and the Paul Brown saga the Department's manifold other activities have had to be financed and carried out throughout the years since 1976.**

25. Not only are a local authority's income and expenditure circumscribed but its powers to incur capital expenditure and to borrow money are subject to statutory control. For example the money required for the adaptation to provide the new Birkenhead Area Office at Grange Mount (see para 43) had to come from what are known as funds for 'Locally Determined Schemes' derived from block allocation from government. Figure 8 shows how the amount available to the Wirral from 'Locally Determined Schemes' has shrunk dramatically over the years, particularly when inflation is taken into account.

26. We consider that, having regard to financial constraints, Wirral Borough Council has allocated money fairly and responsibly to social services and that it wished to increase that allocation. Comparison with other Metropolitan Districts shows that money spent on social services by Wirral was in Mr Wood's words 'Very middle of the road'. Exact comparison between

## Figure 5. Analysis of Social Services Budgets 1976–1981

*£000's*

| | *Base Budget* | | | | | *Final Adjustments* | | *Net Requirements* | | |
|---|---|---|---|---|---|---|---|---|---|---|
| *Year* | *Inflation* | *Committed Expansion* | *Economies* | *Other Variations* | *Total* | *Additions* | *Reductions* | *Social Services* | *All Services* | *Social Services Proportion* |
| | | | | | | | | | | % |
| 1976–77 | 1,173 | 168 | | 258 | 6,353 | 17 | 145 | 6,225 | 55,626 | 11·2 |
| 1977–78 | 1,067 | 58 | | Cr 230 | 7,119 | 202 | 51 | 7,270 | 60,691 | 12·0 |
| 1978–79 | 962 | 49 | | 78 | 8,359 | 123 | — | 8,482 | 65,685 | 12·9 |
| 1979–80 | 801 | 3 | | Cr 25 | 9,261 | 129 | — | 9,390 | 72,584 | 12·9 |
| 1980–81 | 1,589 | 53 | Cr 462 | 95 | 10,665 | — | — | 10,665 | 77,937 | 13·7 |

Figures provided by Finance Department, Wirral Borough Council, April 1980.

## Figure 6. Current Revenue Expenditure Guidelines 1976–1981

| *Year* | *Government Guidelines* | *Wirral Base Budget* | *Final Budget Adjustments* | |
|---|---|---|---|---|
| | | | *All Services* | *Social Services* |
| 1976–77 | Standstill situation. Committed expansion to be financed from savings. Pay increases limited to £6 per week. Introduction of cash limits for grant purposes. | Existing standards of service *plus* additional expenditure arising from contractual commitments. | Restricted list of new revenue items totalling £126,000. Reductions of £972,000 to finance expansion. | Minor expansion of £17,000. Reductions of £145,000 mainly by reducing residential placements. |
| 1977–78 | Reduce current revenue expenditure by 1·6%. (RSG reduced from 65½% to 61%). | Existing standards of service. Employees in post and vacant posts authorised for filling. Effects of contractually committed projects. | Authorised additional items of £470,000 and reductions of £1,517,000 to match minimum target set by Government. | Additional items totalling £202,000. Savings of £50,000 (mainly closure of Holiday Home). |
| 1978–79 | Standstill or breakeven position. | Existing standards of service. Employees in post and vacant posts authorised for filling. Effects of contractually committed projects. | Savings started in 1977–78 expected to produce reduction of £1,323,000 in 1978–79. Savings then redeployed to permit expansion of £1,367,000. | Additional items of £123,000 broadly in line with increase for all services. |
| 1979–80 | Growth of 1·6% in current revenue expenditure. | As above, plus full year's effect of approved economies. | Authorised additional items totalling £1,034,000. | Additional items of £129,000. |
| 1980–81 | Reduction of 5% in the level of expenditure planned for 1980–81. | As above. | Total reductions of £3,066,000 to match the government's guideline. | Pro rata reductions of £462,000 on Social Services. |

Figures provided by Finance Department, Wirral Borough Council. April 1980.

**Figure 7. Analysis of Actual Gross Expenditure Less Total Income 1976–1979**

*£000's*

| | *Expenditure* | | | | | |
|---|---|---|---|---|---|---|
| *Year* | *Residential Services* | *Day Care* | *Other Services* | *Total* | *Less Income* | *Net Expenditure* |
| 1976–77 | 4,063 (54%) | 860 (12%) | 2,563 (34%) | 7,486 (100%) | 1,128 | 6,358 |
| 1977–78 | 4,643 (52%) | 1,080 (12%) | 3,268 (36%) | 8,991 (100%) | 1,499 | 7,492 |
| 1978–79 | 5,458 (52%) | 1,215 (11%) | 3,875 (37%) | 10,548 (100%) | 1,643 | 8,905 |

Figures provided by Finance Department, Wirral Borough Council, June 1980.

**Figure 8. Borrowing Powers for Locally Determined Schemes**

*£000's*

| *Year* | *Wirral's own allocation* | *'Borrowed' allocations* | *Total Available* | *Grange Precinct (LDS only)* | *Other* Schemes* |
|---|---|---|---|---|---|
| 1976–77 | 2,707 | 1,246 | 3,953 | 3,038 | 915 |
| 1977–78 | 1,491 | 400 | 1,891 | 1,498 | 393 |
| 1978–79 | 891 | (50) Repayment | 841 | 725 | 116 |
| 1979–80 | 529 | | 529 | 262 | 263 |
| 1980–81 | 608 | | 608 | — | 608 |

* Expenditure on 'other schemes' relates almost exclusively to commitments inherited from the former authorities (eg West Kirby complex and the Leasowe Sports Centre) together with other inescapable items (eg furniture for Key sector projects included in approved capital programmes for Education and Social Services).

Figures provided by Finance Department Wirral Borough Council June 1980

Authorities is not possible because of the crude nature of the statistics. **At times of financial stringency we consider that the Social Services Committee and the Director of Social Services and his senior management, working together, have an even greater responsibility than usual for ensuring the wise deployment of available resources. In such times the protection of life and the fulfilment of statutory duties must come first.** In this context we note that as part of the 1980/81 savings exercise the Director of Social Services included the freezing of five social work posts. In view of the pressures on the Department we hope that the Social Services Committee can find the means to unfreeze these posts.

**Social Services Reorganisation**

27. **The discharge of social welfare functions, in particular in regard to services provided for children, must be seen in an historical context. It is only thus that the successes and failures of individual social workers can be fairly judged and the events which ended in tragedy for Paul Brown can be assessed.**

28. Prior to the creation of unified Social Services Departments in 1970 'welfare' services were provided by a variety of local government departments. Children's Departments, staffed by child care officers, were responsible for such services as: preventive work with families; reception of children into care; supervision of children in care; fostering and adoption; and juvenile court work. Local Authority Welfare Departments provided a fieldwork service to the elderly, physically handicapped, homeless, blind, deaf and dumb and to problem families, while the Health Departments provided a social work service in the fields of mental health, problem families, unmarried mothers and the after-care of the sick. By combining these and other responsibilities it was hoped to create a Department which could tackle problems on a family basis and which could undertake preventive work. Prior to 1970 family casework and preventive social work were still in their infancy.

29. The Seebohm Committee recognised the need to retain specialist skills at headquarters and even at Area level and did not intend former specialists

to abandon everything on reorganisation, taking on completely new types of work. Rather it was intended that existing skills would be carried over into the new Departments but a combination of a more rational approach to social work and the provision of increased resources would lead to the emergence of the generic social work team. The social services expanded rapidly in the early 1970s but the mid-1970s saw the beginning of the local government expenditure cuts and the planned growth was never achieved. As public expectations increased untrained and inexperienced staff were allocated larger and larger caseloads with problems which they had never before encountered.

**Health Visitors and NHS Reorganisation**

30. Following closely upon the creation of Social Services Departments came preparation for the reorganisations of local government and the National Health Service which both came into effect on the 1st April 1974. The reorganisation of the NHS involved not only a drastic reorganisation of the management structure and the redrawing of boundaries but also, in an attempt to produce a corporate health service, involved the transfer of staff who had previously been employed by other authorities to the new National Health Service. One of these groups of staff was the health visitors who had previously been employed by local authorities.

31. Miss Rowlands who was the Divisional Nursing Officer for Community Nursing Services in the Northern District told us of the very high caseloads of health visitors in the North of Wirral AHA and of the difficulties of recruiting staff to work in North Wirral. Staff tended to drift from North Wirral (an area of high social deprivation) to South Wirral (a more affluent area with far fewer problems) when vacancies arose. Although the establishment for health visitors in Wirral North has been increased from 35·5 whole time equivalents (WTE) in 1976 to 52 WTE in April 1980, the number of staff in post has risen only marginally, from 35·5 WTE in 1976 to 40·25 in April 1980. We understand that general practitioners receive an extra financial payment when working in a designated area and that a similar payment is made to teachers and social workers when working in a priority area. **We consider that a similar salary differential for health visitors should be introduced.**

**Local Government Reorganisation**

32. In the case of local government reorganisation although the shadow authorities, comprising members and chief officers, did not come into being until 1973 planning had begun long before that date. For those Chief Officers who remained in the same geographical area 1973 was a year of running down the old authority while trying to build up the new one. For those Chief Officers who moved to a new area on reorganisation the problems were even greater: with no experience of any of the constituent authorities a new Chief Officer was effectively planning in a vacuum. Further down the hierarchy staff who had been in senior positions in small authorities had to compete against colleagues from the other constituent authorities for those same senior positions in the larger re-organised Departments; this inevitably resulted in staffing problems and disturbance. Conversely, Chief Officers were faced with the difficulties of appointing senior staff from within the pool of existing

employees of the constituent authorities. This meant that someone from a senior position in a small authority could be in a position of greater responsibility in the new larger authority. Staff from small County Boroughs were mixed with others who had worked in the larger Counties and senior management had to reconcile the often very different working methods of the two groups.

**The effects of the reorganisations in Wirral**

33. The difficulties for social workers in adapting to their new post-Seebohm role were exacerbated in the constituent authorities of the Wirral by a significant shortage of staff. The Wirral constituent authorities which had had social services functions were Birkenhead and Wallasey County Boroughs and Cheshire County Council (of which Wirral acquired the Urban Districts of Hoylake and Wirral and the Borough of Bebington). Cheshire and Wallasey had decentralised their social services on Seebohm lines (ie through a system of Area Offices) but Birkenhead had not.

34. **In the local government reorganisation of 1974 the creation of the new Wirral Metropolitan District (under the new Merseyside County Council) was a most complex reorganisation.** (See the map at Figure 9). Parts of the comparatively wealthy Cheshire County (which had a total population of approximately 1,050,000) were linked to the comparatively poor County Boroughs of Birkenhead (approximately 142,000) and Wallasey (approximately 101,000). The headquarters of the new local authority Departments had to be distributed between Birkenhead and Wallasey since neither town could accommodate all Departments. The shadow Chief Officers' group recommended that the Departments to which the public required regular access—mainly Social Services, Housing and Finance (for the rates)—should be accommodated in the 'commercial' centre of Birkenhead with the rest being housed in the less accessible Wallasey Town Hall. But the shadow Council decided that the three central Chief Officers—the Chief Executive, the Director of Finance and the Director of Administration and Legal Services—should be located together in Wallasey. Thus the Social Services Department with its headquarters in Birkenhead was physically cut off from the political and administrative centre of the authority. While this arrangement may have been unavoidable we consider that it increased the problems of the director of Social Services from the very beginning of the new authority.

35. In terms of the effect on individual staff, local government reorganisation resulted in, for example, social workers moving from the modern South Annexe of Wallasey Town Hall into the decidedly unsuitable old Annexe, built in 1947. All furniture and equipment remained in situ and the Social Services Department headquarters in Birkenhead were without a photocopier for some months. On our visits to the Area Offices we saw a wide variety of odds and ends of furniture which, staff told us, had been acquired after reorganisation to make up for the lack of desks, filing cabinets etc. **The combination of the upheaval of the actual move with the poor quality of the accommodation available to the Social Services Department clearly did not help staff morale in the period immediately after the 1st April 1974.** The Chairman of the Social Services Committee condemned the facilities provided. Following

**Figure 9**
**Wirral Peninsula**

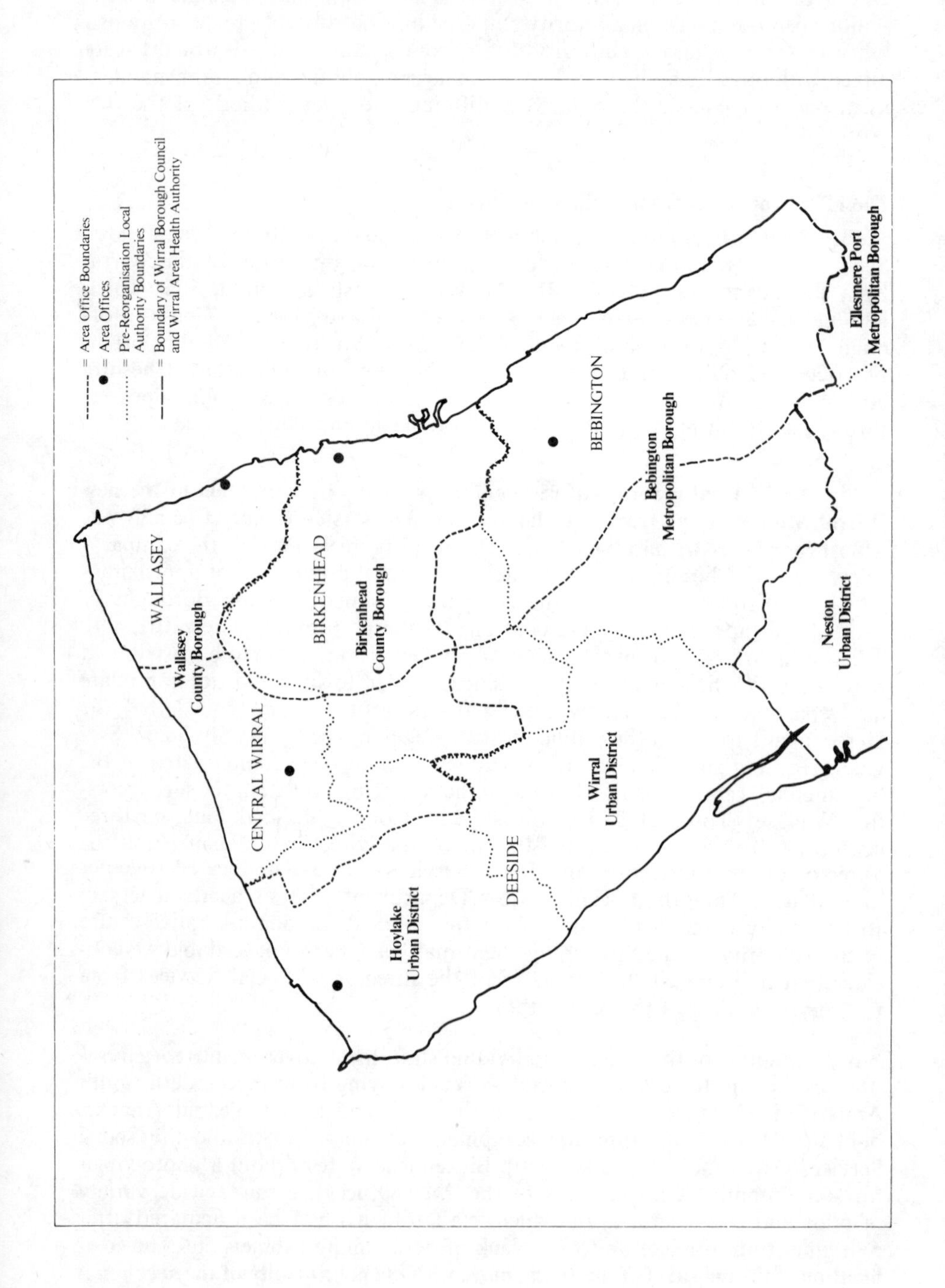

a visit to three of the Area Offices in June 1974 he sent a memorandum to the Director which included the following passage:

> 'Following my examination of the social services departments in Birkenhead, Wallasey and Moreton and discussions with staff at those offices I was horrified to see inadequate furniture, filing cabinets and waiting and interview facilities.
>
> This must be having a grave effect upon our staff and the public.'.

**Despite this comment by the then Chairman of the Committee we found that as recently as July 1980 there had been no significant improvement in the case of Wallasey and it was only in March 1980 that the Birkenhead office moved to new premises.**

36. Another cause of difficulties was the shortage of administrative and clerical staff. Although the social work staff of the old Cheshire County transferred to the new Wirral in many cases the administrative staff did not do so. At a time when experienced administrative staff were vitally needed to harmonise the different procedures of the constituent authorities this shortage was particularly damaging. **Adequate administrative back-up is not a luxury for social workers, it is a necessity.** Social workers should be occupied mainly with their clients—that is where their skills and experience can most profitably be employed—but in the absence of clerical support they are obliged to spend too much of their time on administrative procedures.

37. Gradually the adverse effects of the three reorganisations, most clearly seen in the years 1974 to 1976, are being replaced by the long term benefits. **But at the critical period of March 1975 when difficult decisions requiring experience and knowledge of child care work and law had to be made in the case of Paul and Liam the Birkenhead Area Office had no-one experienced in child care.** The Social Worker responsible for the boys was inexperienced and unqualified. She could only turn for support and guidance to the Area Officer whose background was many years' experience in mental health.

**Social Services Department accommodation**

38. The Area Office of a Social Services Department has special requirements in terms of accommodation which are not always readily appreciated. Although space may be reduced to take account of the fact that social workers are away from the office for much of the day it must also be increased to provide waiting rooms, reception areas, interview rooms and conference rooms. While no office will be perfect, particularly if it is not purpose built, these facilities are requirements rather than luxuries and their absence can affect the quality of social work. We do not advocate accommodation which is cosy for social workers and luxurious for their clients but the accommodation must be appropriate for the work that has to be done. **Adequate accommodation is the necessary tool of the social worker just as machinery is for the factory worker.** The long term aim should be purpose built offices with plenty of sound-proof interview rooms; play areas and creches where children can be kept while their parents are being interviewed; comfortable suitable waiting areas, for the old, handicapped and mothers with children; entrances and passages suitable for the infirm; and offices which are quiet, private and

pleasant enough to enable the staff to make thoughtful judgements in often harrowing cases.

39. We describe below the accommodation occupied by Bebington, Deeside and Wallasey Area Offices and the new Birkenhead Office at Grange Mount. For Central Wirral and the former Birkenhead Office which featured in the Paul Brown case we go into more detail about the accommodation problems and also touch on the staffing of the Offices.

40. The **Bebington** Area Office was the best and most liked of the 5 original Area Offices. Converted from a residential house, with the addition of a single storey annexe, it suffered from the ubiquitous problems of restricted access for the disabled and an inadequate waiting area and like all the offices we saw it was in need of a coat of paint. Apart from these problems we thought the accommodation was reasonable.

41. The **Deeside** Area Office is housed on the top floor of the old Hoylake Town Hall. Part of the former Council Chamber has been partitioned off to provide a dingy reception area and the rest of the Chamber is unused. This room is aptly referred to as 'the barn'. The social work teams are housed in a warren of offices thinly partitioned off from each other. We saw peeling paint, chipped plaster, evidence of damp and bare floorboards covered with odd scraps of carpet. The furniture had an air of 'made do and mend' with sideboards and chests of drawers being pressed into duty as filing cabinets. The long flight of stairs to the reception area must be a particular problem for Deeside's large population of elderly people. While most of these faults do not directly prevent social workers from providing a good service they could have a lowering effect on morale.

42. The description of the **Wallasey** Area Office which we heard from the current Area Officer—Mr Surridge—did not prepare us for the sordid reality. Prior to reorganisation the Area Office had occupied the modern South Annexe to Wallasey Town Hall, with its purpose built ramp for disabled people. The old Annexe, built in 1947 (and not redecorated since according to Mr Surridge), must have been a depressing introduction to the new Wirral for the Wallasey staff who moved there on the 1st April 1974. In the same year the Wallasey Office was visited by HM Factory Inspectorate who gave an adverse report on the premises. We heard evidence of continuing problems with damp and with the wiring, plumbing, heating and security of the building from 1974 until the present day. We saw for ourselves the trailing cables, holes in the floor, chunks of plaster missing from the walls and the evidence of damp. We heard of infestations of woodlice, outcrops of fungus and the persistence of unexplained unpleasant smells. On the 20th May 1980 and on the 3rd June 1980, while our Inquiry was sitting, the Wallasey Area Office was again visited by HM Factory Inspectorate and improvement notices were served on the Director of Social Services in respect of a number of deficiencies in that Office. The Inspectorate's report listed cleanliness, ingress of water, temperature and electrical safety as matters requiring urgent action. We heard that £85,000 had been allocated to remedy the defects identified. **We feel that the Council should not have allowed this state of affairs to continue for so long.**

**In our opinion the Wallasey Area Office accommodation must be brought up to an adequate standard forthwith.**

43. Since March 1980 the Birkenhead Area Office has been housed in the former maternity hospital of **Grange Mount** which we visited. Only part of the building is at present available for use by the Area Office staff. There is still a great deal of conversion and decoration work to be done in the former hospital but we saw great scope for the creation of an Area Office which could act as the base for a variety of activities within the Area. **Mr Shaw, the Director of Development, told us that the work at Grange Mount should be completed by the end of 1980; we consider it essential that there should be no delay in the completion of the work.**

44. The former **Birkenhead** Social Services Department was the first point of contact with Pauline Brown in 1973 and after reorganisation it was the new Birkenhead Area Office which provided Pauline's Social Worker. The extreme problems caused by the Area Office accommodation played their part in the handling of the Paul Brown case and made it more likely that errors would be made. The Area Office was established in 'The Link', a modern building attached to the main municipal offices in Cleveland Street, Birkenhead. The Social Services Department headquarters were located in another building across the road. It was recognised within the Borough Council from an early stage that the Area Office accommodation was not ideal. The Link building was shared by the Area Office staff and staff from the Finance, Education and Housing Departments. Since there was no separate entrance for the Area Office and no waiting area other than the corridor the Area Officer soon began to receive complaints about the noise and disturbance caused by social workers' clients. There were problems too with the lack of parking space for staff and public.

45. Only one of the three Senior Social Workers at Birkenhead had a room of his own and with flimsy partitioning it was impossible to conduct supervision sessions privately. A document prepared by the Birkenhead Social Workers describing their difficulties in organising adequate supervision because of the poor accommodation stated that:

> 'In an attempt to overcome some of these major problems, we have resorted to utilising vacant offices in Headquarters and space in Birkenhead Park, all well in the sunshine but not too good as a rule!'

46. The strength of feeling among the staff about their accommodation led to threats of a walk out in the Autumn of 1974. The social workers wrote to the Chairman of the Social Services Committee and complained, at staff meetings, to higher management. In our opinion their complaints were justified because they rightly recognised that good social work requires adequate accommodation. In a situation such as prevailed at the Link in 1974 there could not be adequate supervision and hence no staff development. Social Workers had to waylay a Senior and seek advice on specific issues whenever they could. In 1974 the Area Officer, Mr Hotchkiss, did not have his own office and he told us that he sat at whatever desk happened to be free at the time. We did however note that in October 1975 whan Mr Wylde took over as Area Officer he reallocated the accommodation so that he and his

Deputy shared an office. Even this arrangement, which continued until March 1980, was far from satisfactory.

47. Good social work practice in Birkenhead was also hampered by the shortage of telephone lines, and initially, the absence of any direct line to the Area Office, but the difficulties with accommodation and facilities were less important in their effect on the service provided than the staffing problems. An adequate number of suitably trained and experienced staff can operate a good service from very inferior premises. This is not to say that facilities are unimportant but if the staff are unsuited to the job and too few in number to carry it out effectively well-designed accommodation will not ensure a good service. In April 1974 the Birkenhead Area Office comprised the Area Officer—Mr Hotchkiss—and 17 social workers, of whom only one (the Deputy Area Officer, Mr Illingworth) was qualified. In addition to Mr Illingworth there were two other Senior Social Workers; of the 14 Social Workers, two were partially sighted and specially trained in problems of blindness and partial sight. Mr Hotchkiss' pre-Seebohm experience was in mental health which it was thought would be an advantage in tackling the major mental health problems which were known to exist in Birkenhead. Unfortunately none of his three Senior Social Workers came from a child care background. Thus the Area with the highest incidence of child care problems in the Wirral lacked a Senior Social Worker with child care expertise.

48. The staffing of the Birkenhead Area Office caused problems within months of reorganisation. Within 6 months the Area Officer had only 12 social workers in post, none of whom were qualified, and although replacements were found there was a high turnover of staff. For a period of 4 months in 1975 Mr Hotchkiss was the only qualified social worker in the office.

49. On the 1st April 1974, when Mr Hotchkiss arrived as the new Area Officer at Birkenhead he faced a daunting task. **Of all the areas within the Wirral Birkenhead presented the most problems. Its population was the highest and its standard of living the lowest; its case load was inevitably the highest and contained a very high proportion of child care cases.** In the period from April 1974 to October 1975 75 per cent of the work of the Birkenhead Area Office involved children; in the North End District it was as much as 91 per cent. This compared with about 40 per cent in the Bebington Area Office to which Mr Hotchkiss later moved. **Most of the social workers were unqualified and many were of limited social work experience; for some of them Birkenhead was strange territory; established posts were unfilled. Despite the high proportion of child care cases the office lacked a Senior Social Worker with child care experience. The office accommodation provided was ill-sited and insufficient. Administrative, clerical and telephone back-up were inadequate.**

50. The new Area Officer, **Mr Hotchkiss,** was a man of courage and loyal to subordinates and superiors. In personality and background he was not at that time suited to the particular task of Area Officer at Birhenhead. He lacked sufficient flexibility to tackle this most difficult assignment. Moreover he seems to have been weighed down by the difficulties which he encountered. Professionally he was without administrative flair and was very limited in outlook. His background was in mental health and his background coloured

his approach to child care cases which provided the bulk of his workload. Mr Hotchkiss had been appointed to Birkenhead for two main reasons. A DHSS study in 1973 had shown that Birkenhead had a high incidence of mental health problems and Mr Hotchkiss' mental health background made him well fitted to tackle these problems. Secondly and perhaps more significantly the new Wirral Social Services Department was anxious to create a 'Wirral identity', as soon as the new authority came into being, to take the place of the old loyalties and different working methods of the constituent authorities. In accordance with this policy it was decided to post senior staff away from their old patches to become Area Officers in new territory. By October 1975 the need to reinforce the Wirral identity was no longer pressing and the urgent need at Birkenhead for senior staff with child care experience had become manifest. In October 1975 there was therefore a change over and all the Area Officers moved, Mr Hotchkiss going to Bebington and Mr Wylde coming to Birkenhead. When Mr Hotchkiss handed over to Mr Wylde the Birkenhead Office was a very unhappy place. The morale of the staff was very low and the incidence of staff sickness was abnormally high because of stress. Many social workers had left and the number in post was well below establishment. Apart from Mr Hotchkiss the only other qualified social worker at Birkenhead in October 1975 was Mr Housden. The inexperienced and unqualified Social Workers worked largely unsupervised; often they received guidance on procedures from those clerical staff who had worked in the former Birkenhead Children's Department.

51. The new Area Officer, **Mr Wylde,** was a very experienced former child care officer who had joined the Birkenhead Children's Department as an administrator in 1949 and had worked in Birkenhead, primarily in the child care services, until reorganisation. Mr Wylde is an easily approachable man who is liked and trusted by his staff. We noted that when Mrs Doran was troubled about the Paul Brown case it was to Mr Wylde that she turned initially for advice (see para 199). When he returned to Birkenhead Mr Wylde brought with him two of his social workers from Deeside. Both these people—and later another social worker from Wallasey—volunteered to join Mr Wylde at Birkenhead at a time when morale at Birkenhead was known to be low. Although he has no formal social work qualifications Mr Wylde has long experience in child care and, since 1971, in social work generally.

52. **Mrs Gurny,** who had been Mr Wylde's Deputy Area Officer at Deeside and moved into the same post at Birkenhead, was also very experienced in child care. Mrs Gurny came into social work in 1960 and holds the Home Office Certificate in Child Care. Prior to reorganisation she worked for the Birkenhead Social Services Department. Although perhaps staff and clients may not always find her easily approachable we found her to be efficient and hard working.

53. From the 13th October, 1975 the Area Officer and his Deputy knew Birkenhead well and their particular experience lay in the field in which that Office had particularly lacked expertise. In addition to these advantages the move of Area Officers coincided with an improvement in the staffing level at Birkenhead. Shortly after his arrival Mr Wylde wrote a report for Mr McDermott (Assistant Director, Fieldwork) summarising his first impressions

of the Office as he found it. We quote from this report because it paints a vivid picture of the difficulties which the staff were facing:

> 'My immediate impression was one of considerable confusion on both the fieldwork and administrative sides . . . . My first few days in Birkenhead have been mainly spent in wading through innumerable files, referrals etc, which were stacked in the 'seniors' office', unallocated or unattended to. No system of priorities appears to have prevailed and one can pull out referrals of many months ago, marked urgent . . . . The present fieldwork area structure comprises two 'casework' teams and an intake team . . . . The situation at takeover was that one team, servicing incidentally the less stressful area, was comprised of a senior, five social workers (reasonably experienced) and two welfare assistants. The other, servicing the North End, Ford Estate, etc, consisted of two new and totally inexperienced social workers and a welfare assistant. The imbalance is obvious and the accumulation of work referred to above is nearly all in this area . . . . .'

54. The second Area Office which featured in the Paul Brown case was **Central Wirral** (sometimes known as Moreton). From the time of reorganisation this Office, like Birkenhead, had serious problems. Soon after reorganisation in 1974 the Area Offices at Central Wirral, Birkenhead and Wallasey were visited by the then Chairman of the Social Services Committee, Councillor Harding, who was horrified at what he found. Overcrowding in the modern Chadwick Street building which housed the Central Wirral Office was so serious that in the Summer of 1975 the Area Office acquired an outpost in a craft centre in Oakenholt Road, the other side of a busy roundabout from Chadwick Street. In the craft centre the social workers were working on trestle tables and folding chairs.

55. On the 25th June 1975 the staff of the Central Wirral Area Office wrote to Councillor Harding to draw his attention once again to the problems of their office accommodation. Their letter listed some of the major problems:

> '1. A split Area Office ie. 2 Social Work teams and Administration in Chadwick Street, 1 Social Work team, Community Liaison Officer, and Home Help Section in Oakenholt Road Craft Centre. This makes accountability and control of resources very difficult.
>
> In our view, the Craft Centre which is purpose built should be returned to its former and correct use.
>
> 2. Serious complications and some duplication with the administration. Mistakes can prove to be most costly.
>
> 3. Serious lack of amenities ie, no rest room, no luncheon facilities, poor toilet arrangements, primitive tea making facilities.
>
> 4. Inadequate waiting area for the public.
>
> 5. No proper interview facilities.
>
> 6. Chadwick Street is not really suitable for disabled persons.
>
> 7. Overcrowded offices and a marked lack of privacy.
>
> 8. An inability to create an area identity or to have good working relationships with all our colleagues'.

The staff of Central Wirral ended their letter with the following statement:

> 'Failure to provide us with the basic essentials of reasonable accommodation causes us not to be able to provide the consumer service the public have the right to expect'.

Councillor Harding replied to this letter on the 3rd July 1975. He was sympathetic to the problems caused to the staff by the inadequate accommodation, but he was unable to offer immediate practical help. He stated that:

> 'Your problems are well known to me and I sympathise with them and wish that I could offer an immediate solution but this will take time to formulate and resolve.
>
> I have posted a copy of your letter to the leader of the Council and will discuss it with him and the Director of Social Services, in the meantime please be assured that we are aware of the situation and I will do my best to be of practical help as soon as I am able'.

56. In March 1976 extra office accommodation was secured for the Area Office in the Chadwick Street building and the Oakenholt Road team were therefore able to return to Chadwick Street. When we visited the Central Wirral Area Office we were astonished to discover that the staff had resorted to raffles within the office to raise money to redecorate the property. It is symptomatic of the selflessness of the staff that the first room to be redecorated was not one of the team rooms used by the staff but the interview room in which the duty social worker interviews clients. We found the rest of the accommodation to be noisy because of the lack of carpets and curtains and subject to extremes of temperature.

57. Over the years since reorganisation Senior Management and the Area Officers at Birkenhead, Wallasey and, to a lesser extent, Central Wirral, have had to devote an excessive amount of time to accommodation problems. We consider that in the years since 1974 the lack of improvement in the intractable problem of Area Office accommodation caused social workers to think that their Department was at the bottom of the 'pecking order' within the authority. This disillusionment contributed to the estrangement between some Area Office staff and the Social Services Department management team. **The inadequate office facilities and shortages of staff (professional and administrative) exacerbated the problems of work of the staff and were all conducive to a high turnover of staff.**

58. We were struck by the very high incidence of sickness both among social workers and health visitors; much of this sickness was of the nervous debility kind. In our opinion this sickness is cogent evidence of excessive work loads, inadequate accommodation, poor morale and, after 1976, the stress caused by the Paul Brown saga.

**Social work training**

59. Many of the social workers involved in the case of Paul and Liam were unqualified. The Certificate of Qualification in Social Work (CQSW), issued by the Central Council for Education and Training in Social Work, is now the only recognised qualification for field social workers. CQSW

courses are run by universities and polytechnics and a large proportion of the students on the courses are on secondment from Social Services Departments. Unfortunately the system of training by secondment is both expensive (since the students are paid their full salaries rather than a grant) and disruptive (since the secondment results in the temporary loss of staff whose work has to be taken over by others). **Where seconded staff are not replaced it is difficult to maintain an equitable deployment between Area Offices and uneven pressures rapidly build up. Mr Douglas Jones told us that it is only in the last year that he has been given approval for the replacement of staff on secondment.** We were pleased to learn of this change in policy.

60. We consider that Social Services Departments should be given a greater say in the content of CQSW courses, particularly in the amount and content of the legal training given to social workers. We were concerned at the general impression given by witnesses regarding their knowledge of the law. We heard of one social worker who had been in post for a very short time and admitted to having no real knowledge of child care law. Quite senior officers had no knowledge of wardship as a method of protecting children. **We consider that all professional training courses should have a considerable input of general law and of the law relating to children.**

61. We were also concerned that at times of public expenditure cutbacks training may be one of the first casualties. We deplore this. Cuts in training budgets can cause immense problems for the future. We believe that more, not less, money should be allowed for training programmes. **We consider that since training by secondment places such a heavy financial burden on local authorities central government should play a greater part in financing such professional training.**

## CHAPTER FOUR

# MARCH 1973—OCTOBER 1975

62. **On the 15th March 1973 Pauline Brown returned to her home town of Birkenhead,** with her son Paul who had been born on the 22nd June 1972. She was 4 months pregnant awaiting Liam's birth. Pauline was born on the 19th July 1952 and was the youngest of Mr and Mrs Streatfield's three children. She was an emotionally immature wayward girl. As a baby she had suffered from meningitis and nearly died which may possibly account for her later instability. At the age of 7 and again at 16 her mother had taken her to a psychiatrist because of behavioural problems. In 1970 at the age of 18 she had married David Brown, the third son of a large Birkenhead family. During the marriage the periods when Pauline and David lived together probably totalled no more than a few weeks.

63. Prior to her return to Birkenhead Pauline and her son had been living in London with a man who was in the habit of throwing her out when he lost his temper. Mrs Streatfield said she had no room for Pauline and the baby in her house and on the 16th March 1973 Pauline and Paul were therefore admitted to the Homeless Families Unit at Balls Road. The warden Mrs Bowen, a State Registered Nurse who had worked at the Unit since 1966, noted that Pauline was in poor health, having received no medical care during her pregnancy, and that she was 'inadequate, irresponsible and demanding'.

64. Mrs Bowen contacted the West Ham Social Services Department in London requesting further information about Pauline and her cohabitee and on the basis of this information it was decided that Pauline should stay in Birkenhead. Over the next nine months social work support to Pauline focussed on the need to find suitable accommodation. On the 2nd April 1973 **Mrs Francis** a Homelessness Officer with Birkenhead Social Services Department, visited Pauline. In accordance with usual practice a social services file had been opened on Pauline and her children. The main document on such a file is the 'running record' maintained by the social worker which records the social worker's actions and comments on the case. While Pauline was in the Homeless Families Unit both Mrs Bowen and Mrs Francis contributed to the running record.

65. Mrs Bowen ensured that Pauline received medical treatment from Dr Owers, the GP who served the Unit, and arranged for Mrs Murphy, the Health Visitor attached to Dr Owers' practice, to advise Pauline on ante-natal care. While Pauline was in the Unit Mrs Bowen received a complaint about Pauline's treatment of her baby from two other residents who suggested that Pauline had viciously attacked Paul and that they had seen finger marks on his back. Mrs Bowen examined Paul and found no signs of bruising. She noted that Pauline was unpopular with the other residents. Mrs Bowen had noted that:

'Pauline has a mental age of about 10 years, she is not able to work to a reasonable routine, things 'happen', cleaning, shopping, baby care, cooking, washing are given only occasional consideration'

and also:

'Pauline is careless in her handling of money, she did not have money to provide food for herself or baby'.

Because of this, when Mrs Francis found Pauline a large bedsit, at 41 Clifton Road, she asked Pauline's mother to help, particularly with the washing and paying the rent. Pauline moved into the bedsit on the 2nd June 1973.

66. Over the next few months Mrs Francis visited Pauline regularly, she arranged for Paul to be received into care when Liam was born (the 7th August 1973) and continued the search for better accommodation. She noted Pauline's difficulties with keeping the place clean and tidy and attributed these to the unsuitability of the bedsit. Mrs Murphy was also visiting and observing Paul and Liam's development. On the 7th October when Liam was 2 months old he was admitted to Alder Hey Hospital because, Mrs Streatfield told Mrs Murphy, he was 'going blue and vomiting'. A pyloromyotomy was performed and the surgeon noted that Pauline was at first unwilling to sign the consent form. Because of his poor home conditions Liam was kept in hospital until the end of the month but three weeks after his discharge Mrs Murphy arranged to have him admitted to Birkenhead Children's Hospital because he was not gaining enough weight. Meanwhile, on the 7th December 1973, Pauline had obtained the tenancy of 18 Carol Gardens, a flat close to her mother's home. Mrs Francis arranged for furniture to be supplied and delivered, along with a supply of towels and bedding.

67. Liam was discharged home on the 1st January 1974 and three days later Mrs Murphy visited and noted that Liam 'appeared to be gaining weight', was well clothed and clean. Also that as he was small and not very responsive he would need to be observed. Mrs Murphy's final entry on the 18th February 1974 stated that Liam appeared to be well and that both children attended clinic regularly. With her move to Carol Gardens Pauline changed GP, to Dr Moore, and with the change in GP she also acquired a new health visitor. Her health visitor records were therefore transferred to Mrs Almond. During March 1974 Pauline visited Dr Moore and informed him that she had been addicted to drugs and had financial problems. As the problem was less medical than social Dr Moore recalls that he referred her to the Social Services Department. There is no record of this referral but the Social Services were already in touch with Pauline through Mrs Francis.

68. As a result of local government reorganisation part of the former Birkenhead Social Services Department was reorganised into the new Birkenhead Area Office of the Wirral Social Services Department. Mrs Francis ceased to be responsible for Pauline's case at this time. The months during which Mrs Francis had the care of Pauline and her two children are illustrative of the value of practical support. **Preventive work of this kind is likely to be of great long term benefit for mothers and children and thus for society as a whole.** Mrs Francis established a rapport with Pauline, helped her to find a home, to brighten it up and to have pride in it, and encouraged Pauline's

relationships with her mother and aunts. By the time Mrs Francis ceased being responsible for Pauline there were reasons for optimism. Her final entry on the running record reads as follows:

> 'Mrs Brown's house is now a home and she is quite proud of it. The children appear better cared for. She appears to have acquired a routine now but still requires a guiding hand . . . .'

The Birkenhead Area Office, because of its inadequate resources, was unable to continue to give regular kindly and practical support and for 6 months no social worker saw Pauline. **The type of help required by Pauline is extremely time consuming and expensive of resources. The Wirral Social Services Department do now provide such help, to a limited extent, through the Homemaker Service which bridges the gap between a home help and a qualified field social worker.** Even the Homemaker Service requires the help of the community and of the client's extended family to have the best prospects of success. Developments on these lines in the long term future are, in our opinion rightly, the aims of Mr Douglas Jones (the Director of Social Services) and his Department. Sadly, by the time that Pauline's case had been reallocated she needed more than practical help and advice.

69. There is no record of any contact with Pauline during April 1974 although on the 15th May an abortive visit was made by Mrs Tiddy, a then unqualified Social Worker from Birkenhead. On the 31st July 1974 Mrs Whelligan, Pauline's aunt, telephoned the Birkenhead Area Office and requested that a social worker call on Pauline and the children. She was concerned about Paul who was often falling and was covered in bruises. The referral was passed to Mrs Tiddy but there is no record of any action having been taken and Mrs Tiddy had no recollection of the referral. During August and September Mrs Sayer, who had taken over from Mrs Almond as the Health Visitor on the case in June 1974, made abortive visits to Carol Gardens.

70. In September 1974 Pauline's case was reallocated and on the 9th September **Mrs Heffer** an unqualified Social Worker, recorded her first involvement with Pauline. Mrs Streatfield rang to ask her to receive Paul and Liam into care. She was looking after the boys because Pauline had been admitted to St Catherine's Hospital with a threatened abortion. Mrs Streatfield's husband was ill and being kept awake by the children. Mrs Heffer noted that she thought Mrs Streatfield was more unwilling than unable to care for her grandchildren. Mrs Streatfield also stated that Pauline's latest boyfriend was physically cruel to the children. Mrs Heffer visited the children who appeared fit and well and found a suitable foster home. On the 10th September Mrs Heffer took the children to have a Free From Infection Inspection prior to the fostering and the Health Visitor noted that Paul had bruising of his left eye. Mrs Streatfield said this was caused by a fall. The same day Mrs Heffer spoke to the ward sister at St Catherine's who said that Pauline was an extremely bad tempered girl, that she was troublesome and that she was upsetting some of the other patients. Mrs Heffer visited the children in their foster home and after Pauline was discharged also took her to see the boys on the 12th September.

71. Mrs Heffer also discussed family planning with Pauline and on the 19th September took her to the Family Planning Clinic. On the way Pauline

related a garbled story about her flat having been taken over by a girlfriend whilst she was in hospital. She said that she wanted a transfer from her flat. Mrs Heffer summarised the situation in her running record as follows:

> 'Pauline is an emotionally immature young woman who appears to function on a superficial level only. Because of her obvious limited intelligence she is prone to aggressive outbursts. She herself states that the slightest thing infuriates her and that she constantly loses her temper. This also applies to her attitude to the children. Although Pauline is irresponsible she has genuine affection for the children and her family. This young woman is attention seeking and demanding and will need a great deal of support and help. *Short term aim*: To ensure that the children are not subject to cruelty either by Pauline or her co-habitees. A nursery place for the children may help the situation. *Long term aim*: To help Pauline become independent, to support and guide her but not to take over her responsibilities'.

The boys were discharged from care on the 24th September and Mrs Sayer saw both children on the 7th October 1974. She noted that Paul seemed rather small for his age, spoke well with a large vocabulary and needed observing. Liam was progressing well, walking and saying a few words. Pauline told her that she was waiting for a divorce and that her husband battered the children. Mrs Sayer also noted that the house was in a mess and the mother irresponsible. Three days later Mrs Heffer made an abortive visit and left a letter asking Pauline to call at the office.

72. Pauline visited the office 10 days later, on the 20th October 1974. The children looked well and although she complained again about the flat Pauline agreed that it had the advantage of being near to her mother. During November Pauline again visited the office complaining about the flat and was told to complete a transfer form. On the 17th January 1975 Pauline visited the office at Birkenhead to say that she had seen the 'father' of the children who wanted them all to return to him. Pauline stated that she was frightened that he would take the children if she did not return. Mrs Heffer reassured her that as the man was not the 'true father' he had 'very little legal rights' and advised her to see a solicitor if the threat was real. The children looked well cared for but Pauline was scruffy. Paul and Liam were seen again on the 5th February 1975 and both appeared well. Once again, Pauline asked for help with a transfer from the flat. A month later, on the 12th March 1975, Pauline called at the office without the children but with a boyfriend. She claimed that the DHSS had accused her of 'fiddling the books' and they would not pay her social security allowance as she had lost her book. Mrs Heffer contacted the DHSS who said that Pauline had already cashed the week's cheque. The next day, the 13th March 1975, Pauline again took the children to the Area Office. Both had colds and Pauline said that they had not eaten for three days. She was given food but appeared disgruntled at not being given money.

73. At 7 pm on **Saturday the 15th March 1975** Mrs Streatfield telephoned the Birkenhead Area Office and spoke to the Duty Officer who on that day was Mrs Tiddy. Mrs Streatfield asked her to visit Paul and Liam as she said they were not being fed. Mrs Streatfield said that a visit from a social worker

would be enough and did not give any more details. Mrs Tiddy promised to call that evening if possible but half an hour later she received another urgent call and was busy until 10 pm. As Mrs Streatfield had not stressed any urgency in the problem relating to Paul and Liam and because Mrs Tiddy was aware that the case was actively known to the Social Services Department she did not visit Pauline. Two days later, on Monday the 17th March 1975, at about 10 am, Mrs Tiddy received a phone call from a lady she assumed to be Mrs Streatfield. The caller asked to speak to Mrs Heffer. Mrs Heffer had recently been off sick and Mrs Tiddy assumed that she was still away but did not make any effort to check this fact. She agreed to pass on a message to Mrs Heffer but forgot to do so.

74. Meanwhile on the same day (Monday the 17th) Mrs Streatfield expressed her concern about Pauline and the children to Mrs Shelah Jones, leader of the Cavendish playgroup (which Paul had attended in August 1973) and wife of a Social Services Committee member. On the next day (Tuesday the 18th March 1975) Mrs Streatfield again discussed the situation with Mrs Shelah Jones and expressed concern that in spite of making two telephone calls no social worker had visited Carol Gardens. Mrs Shelah Jones then contacted Mrs Roberts (Playgroup Organiser in the Social Services Department) who in turn contacted the Duty Officer at Birkenhead who on that Tuesday was Mrs Francis. Mrs Francis passed the message to Mr Hotchkiss, the Area Officer, who said that he would telephone Mrs Shelah Jones but that no action could be promised because of the shortage of staff. Mrs Francis also passed on the message to Mrs Heffer. Mrs Heffer set off to visit Pauline and met her and the children on the way. Both children 'smelt foul' and were crying. Pauline asked that the children be taken into care 'to give her a break'. She admitted to beating the children and added she had been taking drugs and had been 'tripping'. Mrs Heffer asked Pauline to return home while she investigated the possibility of placing the children with foster parents. Mrs Heffer later visited 18 Carol Gardens and noticed that both children had diarrhoea. Pauline agreed that Mrs Heffer could undress and examine the children but there was no evidence of bruising except on Paul's face. Mrs Heffer warned Pauline not to leave the children alone and said the police would be asked to keep an eye on her. Mrs Heffer left to continue her search for foster parents. Mrs Heffer did not inform **Mrs Sayer,** the health visitor, of the boys' condition. **Good communication between health visitors and social workers is crucial in such cases and we find that this lack of communication was an error.** Mrs Heffer visited Pauline again later in the same day and told her of the difficulty of finding foster parents. Later on Pauline and a friend presented themselves at the office and Pauline said that she would not move until the children were taken off her hands. Once again she was sent home and warned that she must not leave the children alone.

75. Meanwhile Mrs Shelah Jones had written to the Director of Social Services asking for action to be taken. The letter was delivered to the Director by her husband on the following morning (Wednesday the 19th March). The Director immediately summoned Mr Hotchkiss and Mrs Heffer to his office. Mr Hotchkiss and Mrs Heffer then visited 18 Carol Gardens and Mr Hotchkiss arranged to admit the boys to care under Section 1 of the Children Act 1948. The boys were admitted to Thingwall Hospital, under the care of Dr

Vernon Jones. Mrs Heffer advised Pauline to seek psychiatric treatment. Mrs Streatfield was telephoned and told what had happened and that evening Mrs Shelah Jones wrote a second letter to the Director.

76. Mrs Shelah Jones' second letter to the Director included a reference to drug abuse at Carol Gardens. This matter was referred to the drug squad by Mr Hotchkiss in a letter dated the 28th March 1975 but his letter did not refer to Pauline's own involvement. The matter was investigated by the police but no evidence of drug abuse could be found. **We were pleased to note the very high standard of co-operation and help that the Social Services Department have received from the Merseyside Police. In particular the regularity and quality of Police attendance at case conferences is to be commended. They arrive well briefed about the children concerned and make positive contributions to the discussions.**

77. Following Mrs Shelah Jones' complaints to the Director Mr Hotchkiss called an Area Office meeting attended by Mr McDermott (Assistant Director, Fieldwork) on Thursday the 20th March. The minutes of this meeting reveal a heated exchange of views between those present and indicate the state of dissatisfaction among the staff. Examples of contributions to the meeting include the following, as recorded in the contemporary verbatim note:

> **Mrs Price**—'Many times have we asked, that this subject re lack of communication be looked into, but nothing has been done—only when a member of the public contacts the Director, do we get any action, and have for the first time seen a representative of the Directorate'.
>
> **Mr Davies**—'This Area Office should be the subject of a National and Local scandal. Everytime we have tried to make a change, in this office, nothing has been done'.
>
> **Mrs Hughes-Jones**—'On two separate occasions I have spoken to you (Mr Hotchkiss) and you were not prepared to listen to me, the problem was a battered baby. Mr Housden did a visit with me, as my own Senior was absent at that time. As a result of this visit with Mr Housden the child was received into care, because it was "at risk".'

Mr Hotchkiss had called the meeting because of the lack of communication on the 17th March but Mrs Tiddy did not admit to having told Mrs Streatfield that Mrs Heffer was off sick.

78. Mrs Tiddy was a young, inexperienced, and unqualified Social Worker. Following Mrs Streatfield's complaint that she had not been attended to with sufficient speed and the transmission of that complaint by Mrs Shelah Jones to Mr Douglas Jones, Mrs Tiddy made what she asserted was a spontaneous and voluntary confession statement which included the following passage:

> 'I am prepared to accept responsibility for any error of judgement in this and the fact that this may have encouraged Mrs Streatfield to think that our Department was not taking any action in this matter'.

We consider that this confession was probably inspired from above and was symptomatic of senior management's reaction to criticism, especially from Councillors. Even assuming that Mrs Tiddy had been guilty of some misdemeanour we think that a pompous written confession record of this type was highly inappropriate. The error should have been dealt with informally and educatively by her Area Officer.

79. Meanwhile Paul and Liam were being treated in hospital. On the 23rd March 1975 the nursing record on Paul at Thingwall Hospital includes the entry 'Daddy hits Mummy, also Daddy made sores on left hand with matches'. We note that no action was taken on Paul's allegations. **Hospital nursing notes can provide a valuable source of information in child abuse cases and we consider that comments of this kind in a nursing record should be investigated.**

80. **On the 24th March 1975 Mrs Heffer wrote to Mr McDermott, asking him to place Paul and Liam's names on the Non-Accidental Injury At Risk Register** (which we hereafter refer to as the At Risk Register). Mrs Heffer did not carry out the standard procedure for At Risk Registration as set out in the Wirral booklet on alerting procedures for non-accidental injury. We consider it highly unlikely that Mrs Heffer was aware of these procedures. No case conference was called because Mrs Heffer did not request Mr McDermott to convene one. Mrs Heffer recorded in her running record that Mrs Sayer had been informed of the Registration but Mrs Sayer has consistently maintained that she was not informed. Mr Hotchkiss also denied that Mrs Heffer discussed the matter of Registration with him.

81. Pauline Brown was admitted to St Catherine's Hospital on the 25th March 1975 for psychiatric treatment. Eventually foster parents were found for Paul and Liam and on the 1st April 1975 the two children were discharged from Thingwall Hospital to the home of Mr and Mrs Shackleton. The children were not given the required medical examination before being fostered, perhaps because they were being discharged from hospital and were therefore assumed to be healthy. Mrs Heffer completed Movement Notices but the Area Health Authority, and Mrs Sayer in particular, denied ever receiving them. (Movement Notices are completed whenever a child is received into care, whenever he changes address while in care, and when he is discharged from care. The Notices are copied to the Area Health Authority so that Health Visitors can keep track of the children on their list). Mrs Sayer recorded on the 4th April 1975 that the children had been discharged from hospital to a foster home but she did not know the new address because Mrs Heffer had refused to divulge the information. Pauline was discharged from St Catherine's Hospital on the 5th April 1975 since there was apparently nothing wrong with her. Mrs Heffer made two abortive attempts to see the children at Mr and Mrs Shackleton's but did not see the children until the 10th June 1975 when she took along Paul's birthday money. She noted in her running record that Pauline had gone to London to see Liam's father and had forgotten Paul's birthday. The children looked extremely well and Mr and Mrs Shackleton stated that they were quite willing to look after the children indefinitely. We consider it unfortunate that this offer was not further considered. Pauline also visited the foster home 3–4 times, the last occasion being around midsummer 1975.

82. Towards the end of June 1975 Pauline called at the Birkenhead Office and saw Mr Housden, Senior Social Worker. Mr Housden, like Mr Hotchkiss,

unfortunately had very limited child care experience. His background was work with the elderly and physically handicapped. He told us that he used to telephone Mrs O'Loughlin, the Area Officer at Wallasey, for advice on child care matters. He was unstinting in the help he gave to others in the office but that help was necessarily limited in child care cases. Pauline told Mr Housden that she wanted to take the children to London and Mr Housden told her that Mrs Heffer would visit. Mrs Heffer then contacted Mrs Streatfield who said that Pauline was not talking to her.

83. **Mrs Sayer** recorded that she saw Pauline on the 20th June and persuaded her not to take the children to London. On the 27th June Mrs Heffer recorded that she spoke to Mrs Sayer who agreed that Pauline should not have the children. Mrs Heffer then visited Pauline and persuaded her to leave the children with Mr and Mrs Shackleton. She also told Pauline that she would be leaving at the end of the month and that another social worker would be visiting her. Mrs Heffer's final record was:

> 'This young woman needs constant supervision, especially when she has her children back, as she is so immature and irresponsible'.

**The time for decision**

84. **On Wednesday the 19th March 1975 the Birkenhead Area Office had to take a decision about the future of Paul and Liam. This decision required an assessment of all the information available to the Social Services Department and other agencies. We find that such an assessment was not made; had it been made, the following information should have been assembled:**

a. Mrs Bowen had recorded Pauline as having a mental age of 10 and being unable to establish a routine—'things happen';

b. In September 1974 Mrs Streatfield had claimed that Pauline's latest boyfriend was physically cruel to the children;

c. Mrs Heffer had recorded Pauline as emotionally immature and prone to aggressive outbursts, and had referred to the need to ensure 'that the children are not subjected to cruelty';

d. Pauline had admitted, on the 13th March 1975, that the children (then aged 2 years 9 months and 1 year 7 months) had not eaten for 3 days, Mrs Bowen had touched on this problem and Mrs Streatfield confirmed the March 1975 incident;

e. Pauline had failed to seek medical and ante-natal care when pregnant with Liam;

f. Pauline had admitted to her GP that she had been addicted to drugs;

g. One of Pauline's aunts (Mrs Whelligan), had been worried about bruises on Paul and his hair falling out in July 1974 but no action had been taken;

h. Mrs Patrick, another of Pauline's aunts, had visited Carol Gardens one evening and found the children in bed, alone in the flat. The door was tied shut with string and an electric fire was on. Pauline did not return until midnight. (Mrs Streatfield told us that Pauline's neighbours had reported a similar incident to the police);

i In March 1975 Mrs Patrick had visited the flat and turned out a group of teenagers who were there with Pauline and the children. Paul and Liam looked unkempt and she had returned home to bring food for them. It was this incident which had led Mrs Streatfield to ring the Social Services Department on Monday the 17th March 1975;

j. Pauline had told Mrs Sayer in October 1974 that her husband 'battered the children';

k. January–March 1975 had seen a crescendo of activity on the part of Pauline with requests for a move, requests for money, a claim that her husband might remove the children, failure to feed the children, a claim that she was on drugs and not responsible for what she would do next, and a claim that she had bruised Paul's face.

We find that if all this information had been considered and where necessary investigated and substantiated with the help of relatives and other agencies a case should have been made by the Birkenhead Area Office to assume parental rights over Paul and Liam under Section 2 of the Children Act 1948. We believe that the reason why an application for assumption of parental rights was not made was that Mr Hotchkiss, with his mental health background and lack of experience in child care cases, was convinced that Pauline was bluffing and using emotional blackmail to persuade the Area Office to receive her children into care. Mr Hotchkiss' view cannot however be sustained, on the evidence available at that time. On any view of the matter Pauline's attitude was a clear cry for help and a sign that the children were at risk. **We have no doubt that the local authority should have assumed parental rights over Paul and Liam at this stage.** A second opportunity to consider Paul and Liam's long term future occurred when Pauline first asked for the return of the children in June 1975 (see para 82). In addition to the information available in March 1975 the Social Services Department could, by June 1975, have looked for information from Thingwall Hospital, which would have records on Paul and Liam, and from St Catherine's, which would have a record on Pauline. Three months after she had been pressing the Department to take the children off her hands Pauline now wanted them back. **We consider that as soon as Pauline made her views known there should have been a review of the long term future of Paul and Liam.** In fact this would have coincided with the review required under the Boarding Out Regulations. This statutory duty was not fulfilled.

85. Mrs Heffer left the Social Services Department in June 1975 and the case was not re-allocated until November 1975. Paul and Liam were however seen by another social worker, **Mrs Hughes-Jones,** who was visiting other children placed with Mr and Mrs Shackleton. On the 1st August Mr Shackleton expressed concern about Pauline to Mrs Hughes-Jones. Pauline had visited the children and said that she was going to London with her husband and was going to take the children. Mr Shackleton had telephoned Mrs Streatfield who had begged him not to let the children go. At the time of her visit Mrs Hughes-Jones was under the impression that Paul and Liam were subject to a care order. She told Mr Shackleton that he should refuse to let the children go with Pauline and promised to obtain a copy of the care order. Mrs Hughes-Jones spoke to Mr Hotchkiss about the matter and was told

that the children were not on a care order, and that in his view Pauline was bluffing and had no intention of removing the children. Mrs Hughes-Jones then offered to take over the case but Mr Hotchkiss told her that he intended to re-allocate the case shortly and in the meantime he was looking after the case himself and would see to the matter. Mr Hotchkiss had no recollection of this conversation; we nevertheless accept Mrs Hughes-Jones' evidence as accurate. **We find that this was another opportunity to secure the future of Paul and Liam, by assuming parental rights, which was missed.**

**The At Risk Register**

86. When Mrs Heffer wrote to Mr McDermott asking him to put Paul and Liam on the Wirral At Risk Register in March 1975 there were no clear criteria laid down as to who should be put on the Register, nor what should be done when a child was Registered. These were common problems throughout the country at that time. No case conference was called; no regular review of Registered children was held; no red flash or red star was put on the case file. In 1975 the system was not working as a Register should. Since then major changes have occurred. First Mrs Penk and since March 1979 Mr Matthews have worked on updating the Register. **We consider that the utmost priority should be accorded to the speedy completion of this important task so that the Register becomes an effective tool in the prevention of child abuse.** Mr Matthews now has 'over 400 children from 266 families on the Register. There is a case conference before any child is put on or taken off the Register and each case is reviewed every six months. There is now a Special Child Care Team, headed by Mr Matthews, with 4 qualified Social Workers taking on a small number of families whose children are at great risk. At present the At Risk Register seems to work well.

## CHAPTER FIVE

# OCTOBER 1975—FEBRUARY 1976

87. Soon after her return to Birkenhead (as a result of the move of Area Officers in October 1975) **Mrs Gurny** became involved in the case of Pauline Brown. On the 27th October 1975 Pauline had been admitted to St Catherine's Hospital with abdominal pains. The Hospital Social Worker, Mrs Neal, took a social history from Pauline which was substantially a fabrication on Pauline's part. Pauline had been causing trouble on the word and upsetting other patients by discussing her sex life; according to Mrs Neal she 'more or less' admitted that she was a prostitute and had no other living. Mrs Neal also talked to Mrs Streatfield about Pauline and they both tried to persuade her to stay in hospital until medical investigations were completed. Pauline insisted on discharging herself on the 29th October promising that she would stay the night with a friend and visit the Social Services Department next morning. Mrs Neal therefore telephoned Mrs Gurny to explain the position and at the same time passed on her own notes on the case. **Mrs Neal's action in sending a copy of her report to Mrs Gurny seemed to us a good example of helpful communication between hospital and field social workers.**

88. Pauline did not keep her appointment with Mrs Gurny and **sometime in November 1975 Mrs Gurny allocated the case to Mrs Thornton.** In addition to acting as Deputy Area Officer Mrs Gurny was the Senior Social Worker for the North End team and Mrs Thornton was a member of her team. The file on Pauline had been unallocated since Mrs Heffer had left in June 1975 although Mrs Hughes-Jones had been seeing Paul and Liam on her regular visits to other children fostered with the Shackletons. Mrs Thornton impressed us as a sensible mature person. In 1975 she had no formal social work qualifications but she was a State Registered Nurse, had obtained Part I of the qualification for State Certified Midwife and held a diploma in Paediatric Psychiatry. She had also had four years experience in the Psychosomatic unit in the Royal Liverpool Children's Hospital. She had however been with the Social Services Department for only five months when she was allocated the case by Mrs Gurny.

89. Mrs Thornton recalled that Mrs Gurny gave her the file on Paul and Liam on its own and not as part of a bundle of reallocated files. Neither could recall whether Mrs Neal's papers were on the file and we find that Mrs Thornton never saw Mrs Neal's report. Soon after being allocated the case Mrs Thornton made her first and only visit to the Shackletons. She found Paul and Liam to be well and happy and the Shackletons willing to care for them permanently. **Once again an opportunity to consider Paul and Liam's long term future was not followed up.** Mrs Gurny recalled that there was not much discussion of Paul and Liam at this time and they were not regarded as a cause of 'prime anxiety'. Although Mrs Thornton was now the social worker on the case Mrs Hughes-Jones continued to take an interest in Paul and Liam in her regular visits to see other children boarded out with the Shackletons, who had moved from West Kirby to Wallasey in December 1975. On New Year's Eve Liam fell and cut his chin on a toy drum and eventually had to be admitted to Alder Hey Hospital. Mrs Shackleton told

Mrs Thornton that Pauline had been notified that Liam was in hospital. The Shackletons had not seen Pauline since the summer of 1975 but Pauline's mother had been visiting fairly regularly before the move. Pauline could therefore have obtained the Shackletons' new address from her mother or from Mrs Shackleton herself, a fact of which Mrs Gurny was unaware and which was to be of significance later.

90. By the 1st January 1976 the second statutory review of Paul and Liam required by the Boarding Out Regulations should have taken place. It did not take place; if it had done all the information available should have been assessed.

91. **On the 3rd February 1976 Pauline visited the Birkenhead Office** where Mrs Thornton met her for the first time. Pauline told Mrs Thornton that the unsettled period of her life was now over, she was living with a man of 67 and wanted the children back so that she could establish a home for the family with Liam's father in the Liverpool Seamen's Hostel. She also said that she was divorced from David Brown (which was subsequently found to be untrue) and no longer wandered about the docks or took drugs. Mrs Thornton consulted Mr Wylde and Mrs Gurny and returned to tell Pauline that she would have to visit the address which Pauline had given. Mrs Gurny thought the request for the return of the children was a passing phase and that given a little time Pauline might redirect her attentions 'as she had clearly done in the past'. Mrs Thornton told us she had asked the advice of Mrs Gurny regarding the legal position of Pauline vis-a-vis the children and was told the children were in care under Section 1 of the Children Act 1948 and therefore Pauline could not be prevented from removing them. Two days later Mrs Thornton telephoned Mrs Shackleton and told her of the interview with Pauline. Mrs Shackleton was concerned at Pauline's desire to have the children back; she felt it was a whim and Pauline was not a caring mother.

92. On the 10th February Pauline again visited the Birkenhead Area Office—this time with her husband David. They were insistent that they should have the children. Mrs Thornton again sought the help of Mrs Gurny and Mr Wylde who reiterated the need for the Department to be satisfied as to the accommodation before the children would be discharged. This was intended to be a delaying tactic. Mrs Thornton asked whether or not some legal action might be taken. Mr Wylde repeated what Mrs Gurny had said on the 3rd February—namely that the children were in care on a voluntary basis and Pauline therefore had the right to remove them from care. Mrs Thornton told us that at that time she had heard of the legal powers of the local authority in respect of children in care, but did not know the implications of those powers. She was therefore not in a position to question the advice given to her by her senior officers, neither of whom had read the file; Mr Wylde and Mrs Gurny were relying entirely on what Mrs Thornton told them. Unfortunately Mrs Thornton was unsure whether she herself had read the file prior to Pauline's visit to the office on the 3rd February although she felt sure she must have read it after that interview. Mr Wylde had very little information on the history of the case but was, as he saw it, responding to a situation where the parents had no suitable accommodation to which to take the children if they were discharged from care. He saw his role as

being the 'authority' figure to prevent the children being removed from care. He, like Mrs Gurny, assumed that Pauline did not know the address of the foster parents and therefore did not consider the possibility that Pauline might simply go and remove the children. The outcome of this interview was that Pauline and David agreed to Mrs Thornton visiting them in about a week's time at the address they had given.

93. **The second statutory review required under the Boarding Out Regulations had not taken place. After Pauline's second visit to the office there was therefore an even greater obligation on the Senior Social Worker and the Social Worker to examine together the file and the information obtained from Mrs Neal.** If such an examination had taken place it would have revealed the information listed in paragraph 84 together with the following matters:

a. Pauline's request in June 1975 to take the children to London;

b. The Shackletons' willingness to care for Paul and Liam long term;

c. The evidence of the two visits to the Area Office by Pauline in February 1976; and

d. Pauline's prostitution.

Pauline frankly admitted to us that she had been a prostitute for some years. We believe that if court proceedings had been taken in 1975 or 1976 in relation to Paul and Liam the court would have been satisfied that Pauline was, in those years, an active prostitute which by reason of the manner in which she acquired clients would have endangered Paul and Liam. **All the information listed above should have been assessed and an application for Assumption of Parental Rights should have been made.** We believe that Pauline might well not have challenged such an application and once parental rights had been assumed the onus would be on Pauline to show how conditions had improved sufficiently for her to have the children back.

94. On the 14th February, four days later, Pauline and David returned to Birkenhead Area Office again demanding the return of the children. They were in an aggressive and belligerent mood and because of this Mrs Thornton again sought Mr Wylde's help. Because of the inadequate office accommodation, the interview with Pauline and David had to take place in a public corridor. As well as being aggressive and belligerent Pauline cried with temper. She did most of the talking and was regarded as the dominant character, having 'tremendous influence' over David; within a short period she was able to get him as angry as she was. Pauline knew the children were in care on a voluntary basis and said 'we let you have the children and now we can have them back . . .'. Mr Wylde again stressed the need for the Department to ascertain the address and conditions to which the children would be taken. Mrs Thornton pointed out that in the last ten days Pauline had given three different 'heads of household' and three different addresses to which the children would be taken and that this was a matter of concern. Mr Wylde tried to calm them down by discussing what could be done to meet their request in a proper manner and again suggested that Mrs Thornton should visit the address to which they intended to take the children. The address now being given was the home of David's mother on the Woodchurch Estate. A visit was arranged for the following week. The Browns were clearly not

very happy at the outcome of the interview and left the office saying they intended to see a solicitor.

95. Mrs Thornton informed the Shackletons of the three visits from Pauline and told them that Pauline and David might appear at any time to demand the return of the children. Mrs Thornton told the Shackletons that if Pauline was unaccompanied by a social worker they were to refuse to allow her to remove the children and they were to telephone the Area Office. Having heard this news Mr and Mrs Shackleton decided to alert the local police. They felt they could handle the situation if Pauline arrived alone but not having met David they were unsure what to expect. They therefore alerted the police to ensure prompt action if David proved aggressive or violent.

96. **On the 17th February 1976 Pauline and David arrived at Mr and Mrs Shackleton's home to remove the children from care.** Mr Shackleton explained that he was instructed not to let the children go unless Pauline was accompanied by a social worker. Pauline disagreed with him and Mr Shackleton rang the Birkenhead Area Office as instructed. Mrs Thornton was off sick that day and Mr Wylde was on leave. Mr Shackleton therefore spoke to Mrs Gurny. Mrs Gurny told Mr and Mrs Shackleton that the children were in care on a voluntary basis and the Department could not 'if pushed absolutely to the wall' refuse to discharge Paul and Liam to the care of their mother. If Pauline was insistent on removing the children she should be told she was doing so against the advice of the Department. Mrs Gurny told us that she had no serious reason to believe the children would be in active physical danger but she thought the children would not have such a good standard of care with Pauline and David as they had at the Shackletons.

97. Mr and Mrs Shackleton attempted to persuade Pauline and David to leave the children with them but to no avail; it was quite clear to them that Pauline and David intended to take Paul and Liam. It was also clear that back up and support from the Social Services Department would not be forthcoming. David Brown was unable to arrange transport to his parents' home and as Mr and Mrs Shackleton felt that they had done all they could to dissuade Pauline from taking the children Mr Shackleton took them to the address given by David. He later spoke to Mrs Gurny on the telephone, told her what had happened, and gave her the address on the Woodchurch Estate to which the children had been taken. He understood the address to be that of one of David's brothers (David's parents being out at the time). Mr Shackleton offered to take Mrs Thornton to the place where he had dropped Pauline, David, and the children and identify the house into which they had gone but this offer was not taken up.

98. Mr and Mrs Shackleton were very experienced foster parents, having fostered for a period of eleven years for authorities in Liverpool and the Wirral. It had been their experience that on the discharge of a child from care—whatever the child's legal status—there had always been a social worker from the supervising authority present. In view of their experience and Mrs Thornton's assurances there was good reason for them to believe—erroneously as it turned out—that in the event of Pauline and David arriving to remove the children the Social Services Department would be of assistance. **We con-**

**sider that the Shackletons, as authorised foster parents, had every right to expect that a social worker would come to their home as soon as they telephoned to say that Pauline and David were on their doorstep demanding the return of the children.**

99. On her return to the office Mrs Thornton learnt of the events of the 17th February and because of the Shackletons' concern for Liam's chin she rang **Miss Lloyd, a Health Visitor** at the Woodchurch Health Centre, and asked her to visit. Mrs Thornton gave the two addresses where Liam might be found and Miss Lloyd promised to visit to establish where the boys were living and check Liam's dressing. Mrs Thornton used Miss Lloyd as a means of locating Paul and Liam's address but it was primarily Mrs Thornton's responsibility to find the boys and to visit them in their new home to check that it was satisfactory. Only then should she have passed on the case to the Central Wirral Area Office, in whose area the boys were now living. Mrs Thornton thought she had made it clear to Miss Lloyd that Paul and Liam's move was a permanent one and therefore assumed that Miss Lloyd or one of her colleagues would continue visiting. Miss Lloyd gained the impression that the boys were only staying with their 'grandparents' for a short visit and that her role was to pay a 'one off' call. She visited and found the boys living with David's parents at 43 Grasswood Road, Woodchurch. By coincidence Miss Lloyd visited 43 Grasswood Road at the same time as Dr Vaughan Roberts, the GP to whose practice she was attached. This coincidence of visits had arisen because Pauline had complained of abdominal pains and Sarah Brown, being unable to get Pauline's own GP (Dr Moore), had asked her own GP, Dr Vaughan Roberts, to treat Pauline as a temporary patient. Dr Vaughan Roberts arranged for Pauline to be admitted to hospital. He did not recall seeing Paul and Liam on this visit. On the 19th February, the day after her visit, Miss Lloyd rang Mrs Thornton and confirmed the children's new address. She reported that the children appeared well, adequately nourished and generally happy, that Sarah Brown had dressed Liam's chin satisfactorily and the wound appeared to healing well. She also reported that Pauline's pupils were dilated.

100. Meanwhile **Mrs Sayer,** the health visitor working from the Conway Health Centre, was recording abortive visits to Pauline's address in Carol Gardens. She recorded 4 such visits in November 1975, two in January 1976, two in February and one in March. The purpose of her intended visits was to discuss with Pauline her general state of health. She assumed that the children were still with their foster parents during this time, hence the focus on Pauline.

101. Visits on which a health visitor or social worker is unable to gain access, or when the client is unwilling to let the case worker in, assume particular significance in child abuse cases. Such visits should therefore be accurately recorded and their significance appreciated and discussed with superiors. **A repeated failure to gain access should in itself be a cause for concern and should prompt the case worker to check whether other agencies are experiencing the same problem and, where necessary, initiate the appropriate action.**

102. Mrs Thornton spoke to the Ward Sister at St Catherine's Hospital where Pauline had been admitted on the 19th February and discussed the possibility of checking whether Pauline was taking drugs. She did not follow this up with the hospital. Subsequently Mrs Thornton telephoned Mrs Streatfield who expressed concern that the children had been removed from care and undertook to inform Mrs Thornton of any change of address of Pauline. Mrs Thornton's final comment on her records before transferring the file to the Central Wirral office was:

> 'The situation is very unsatisfactory and close observation of the family is essential, taking into account reports of previous neglect'.

**The use of case files**

103. One of the most disturbing features of this case is the failure of a number of staff, either directly or indirectly involved, to read the case file. **We are of the view that if the case file had been fully written up and studied more closely the course of events might have been different.** An example of the dangers which follow from not reading the file can be seen in the assumption by some senior staff that Pauline did not know the address of her children's foster parents.

**Legal powers for the protection of children**

104. Since we believe that some action should have been taken on or before the 17th February to secure the safety of Paul and Liam we considered what would have happened if someone from the Birkenhead Area Office had asked the Department of Administration and Legal Services (DALS) for advice on the 17th February 1976. At this time the solicitor from the DALS who provided advice to the Social Services Department was Mr Betteridge. In his evidence Mr Betteridge told us that in 1976 it was his view that the local authority did *not* have a duty to return a child in voluntary care with foster parents to the natural parents, if this action would be inimical to the welfare of the child. If Mrs Gurny had asked for his advice on the case of Paul and Liam in February 1976 he would have advised that the Shackletons did not have to return the boys to Pauline but that the Department should make a speedy application to assume parental rights. Mr Betteridge frankly admitted that he would not have recommended **wardship** procedure. Wirral Borough Council's first experience with wardship did not arise until 1978—in the case of J v J. The Children Act 1948 and subsequent legislation provide the usual legal framework for the local authority in the discharge of its responsibilities in relation to children. If this framework does not provide adequate protection for a child the local authority should consider using the **wardship procedure which may fill the gap, particularly in difficult and unusual cases.** The great strengths of wardship are the speed with which it can become operative and its flexibility. The judge has wide discretionary powers to impose conditions as to care and control, residence and supervision.

105. We noted the comments regarding assumption of parental rights in the Director of Social Services' report on the Paul Brown case which was prepared for (but never submitted to) the Social Services Committee in 1977 which states:

'. . . but to deprive parents of their rights to their children is an extremely serious step to take and not one which is usually taken when children have been in care for such a short period'.

We would wish to make two comments on this statement. Firstly, whilst a Social Services Department exists to help people in trouble or difficulty it must be emphasised that in respect of children the Department is also a protection agency and the rights of the parent must always be balanced against the need to protect the child. A number of social work staff in giving evidence referred to the rights and responsibilities of parents. **We would wish to draw attention to the rights of children to be protected from those parents who, for whatever reason, expose their children to influences which impair their proper development.** In our view such was the position with Pauline. We also wish to stress that the protection of children by assuming parental rights is not governed by the length of time during which the child has been in care. **Pauline Brown had not provided Paul and Liam with an emotional or physical environment conducive to their development. There was therefore no need to wait for some unspecified length of time before securing the children's future. We believe this would best have been done by the local authority asuming parental rights over Paul and Liam soon after they came into care in March 1975.**

106. The events of February 1976 illustrate the importance of a good liaison between Social Services Departments and Legal Departments. Although we believe that social workers should be given a basic knowledge and understanding of the legal aspects of their work as part of their social work training, they will inevitably need to seek the advice of a solicitor from the Legal Department from time to time. We consider that the responsibility for advising a Social Services Department on child care legislation should be given to a senior solicitor with a particular knowledge of and interest in the care of children. The solicitor should know which facts are relevant in a legal context and he should give advice on obtaining evidence. He must realise that when a crisis occurs the social worker has to move fast. It is therefore important that someone from the Legal Department should always be available to give advice in the event of an emergency. The Social Services Department should inform the Legal Department of their policy in relation to children. The Legal Department should inform the Social Services Department, with explanatory notes, of any relevant recent child care court cases, changes in the relevant statutes, or legal articles, so that the Director can ensure that his staff are kept up to date on the law as it affects their work.

107. It is perhaps worth summarising here the comparatively simple administrative procedure involved in the assumption of parental rights, under Section 2 of the Children Act 1948, as it obtains in the Wirral. First, a report giving the history of the case and the grounds for assuming parental rights is presented to the special sub-committee of the Social Services Committee. The sub-committee makes a decision to assume parental rights and a notice is served on the parents giving them one month in which to give notice of objection to the resolution. If there is no objection the resolution stands and the Council has parental rights over the child. The parents can agree, in writing, to the passing of a Section 2 resolution. If the parents object the Council will receive a notice objecting to the resolution and the case must then be

brought before the court within 14 days. The court hears the case and makes a decision. If the court finds for the parents the resolution lapses; if for the Council, the resolution stands. The special sub-committee can at any time rescind a resolution assuming parental rights simply by so resolving. This can be done on its own volition or at the request of the parents. If the sub-committee rescinds the resolution the child could revert to Section 1 status (ie in care voluntarily) or, which is more likely, be discharged or removed from care. The parents can at any time ask the sub-committee to rescind a Section 2 resolution and if the sub-committee refuses the parents can make application to the Juvenile Court for the case to be heard. The onus is then on the parents to prove that the situation which gave rise to the resolution has changed.

## CHAPTER SIX

# FEBRUARY 1976 — AUGUST 1976

108. On **The 23rd February, 1976** Stanley, Pauline and David visited the local office of the Department of Health and Social Security to claim increase of benefit for the care of Paul and Liam. One of the staff at the DHSS Office thought he could smell drugs on Pauline and David and informed Mrs Thornton. Mrs Thornton phoned the Central Wirral Area Office, which covered the Woodchurch Estate, to tell them of the transfer of the case; she spoke to a clerk typist and was told that Mr Alan Davies would be allocated the case, as he was already familiar with other members of the Brown family. From the 25th February until mid March 1976 Mrs Thornton was off sick and in her absence Mrs Horsfall, clerk typist to her team, wrote to Central Wirral (on the 27th February) transferring the file on Pauline, Paul and Liam and asked for a receipt. Mrs Horsfall also completed Movement Notices recording Paul and Liam's change of address but these never reached the health visitors. Mrs Neal's notes on Pauline were still separated from the file and were not sent to Central Wirral until the 12th March 1976.

109. At this stage the file of Pauline, Paul and Liam was one file and its whereabouts during the next three months had important implications. The index card at Birkenhead is marked 'File sent to Central Wirral 27.2.76' in the handwriting of a clerk, Mrs Dilys Jones. On the 8th March 1976 Mrs Rainford, a clerk typist at the Central Wirral Office, typed at the bottom of the receipt form for another client's file 'Also file received: Mrs Pauline Brown, 43 Grasswood Road, Woodchurch'. This receipt was lost in the files at Birkenhead and only rediscovered during our Inquiry. An index card was filled in by Mrs Rainford and on this card the case is marked as allocated to Mr Pickstock. At that time the card did not have on it a red star, as required, to indicate that the children were on the At Risk Register. Despite the receipt dated the 8th March the file was not seen by any social worker at Central Wirral until May 1976. Both Mr Evans (Area Officer) and Mr Pickstock visited the Birkenhead office on more than two occasions in March and April seeking the file. In May Mr Pickstock found the file at Birkenhead with a note attached saying that it had been sent to the wrong office. The receipt form on the file was marked 'Mr K Wild Birkenhead' and the file had therefore been inadvertently returned to that office. At the beginning of March 1976 the team in which Mr Pickstock worked were moving office from Oakenholt Road to Chadwick Street. Files were stacked on the floor or on tables at Chadwick Street and were not sorted out for several weeks. It would not have been difficult for a file to have gone astray at that time. The present system for the transfer of files is described in paragraph 141.

110. At about the time of Paul and Liam's move **Mrs Sayer** was trying to find out where the children were living as she realised she had not seen them for some time. She rang Birkenhead Area Office and spoke to six social workers, who, although they tried to be helpful, were not able to find the address to which the children had gone. We note that despite Mrs Sayer's attempts throughout the period when Paul and Liam were in foster care to

obtain the foster parents' address there were a number of sources which she left untapped, including Thingwall Hospital and Pauline herself.

111. **Late in the afternoon of Friday the 5th March 1976 Mrs Costello, a Senior Social Worker at Central Wirral, received a phone call from Mr Wylde to say that Paul and Liam's grandmother had phoned to warn him that Pauline intended taking the children to London where they would be homeless.** Mr Wylde suggested that a Place of Safety Order was required. At the time Mr Wylde thought it was Mrs Streatfield, Pauline's mother, who made this phone call but we find that it was Mrs Sarah Brown. Mrs Costello instructed Mr Pickstock, an unqualified Social Worker on her team, to take out a Place of Safety Order.

112. **Place of Safety Orders**

Briefly, the purpose of a Place of Safety Order is to enable anyone in an emergency to protect a child or young person who is believed to be 'At Risk'. There are a number of statutory provisions under which such an order may be made. Any person may apply for an order if he can show he has reasonable cause to *believe* one of the grounds in Section I of the Children and Young Persons Act 1969 exists. There are differences in procedure for the police and social work agencies but the purpose is the same, namely the protection of a child or young person. A Place of Safety is defined as meaning a community home, police station, hospital, surgery or any other suitable place, the occupier of which is willing to receive the child or young person.

113. **Mr Pickstock went to 43 Grasswood Road and served the Place of Safety Order on Pauline,** with a copy to Sarah. The reason for obtaining the Place of Safety Order had been that Pauline was going to take the boys to London but when Mr Pickstock arrived at the house Pauline was about to go into hospital because of a suspected miscarriage. Mr Pickstock served the Place of Safety Order nonetheless, to ensure that Pauline would realise that even when she come out of hospital she should not take the two boys to London. Stanley and Sarah agreed to look after the boys indefinitely and to let Mr Pickstock know if Pauline returned to Grasswood Road after her discharge from hospital.

114. Although the situation had changed since Mr Wylde's last involvement with Pauline some four weeks earlier we were surprised that Mr Wylde recommended a Place of Safety Order on the grounds that Pauline might take the children to London. It was known to the Birkenhead office in February 1976 that Pauline had given 4 different addresses to which she intended to take the children. This, coupled with Pauline's known unreliability and untruthfulness, should have been taken into account by the Birkenhead Office during the period when Pauline was demanding the return of her children, and preventive legal action should have been taken then. In our view the grounds for care proceedings in March 1976 were not as strong as the grounds for assumption of parental rights or wardship had been earlier.

115. **On Tuesday the 9th March 1976 Mr Pickstock visited 43 Grasswood Road** again to make sure that Pauline had not returned. He saw both children who were well and happy and learnt that Pauline, who had left hospital, was staying with a brother-in-law (whose child, as the Office later discovered, was on the At Risk Register) in Fernybrow Gardens about 100 yards away. Pauline had not made any contact with Paul and Liam. Mr Pickstock then reported back to Mrs Costello and they agreed that the Place of Safety Order should be allowed to lapse. Care proceedings were not considered at this time, nor at any time in March 1976, as it was felt that the Browns were a suitable family to look after children although Mr Pickstock neither examined the home nor consulted the office files on the Browns. This opinion was confirmed on **the 19th March when Mr Pickstock visited again.** Mr Pickstock had agreed to prepare an addendum for a court report which Mr Alan Davies had written about six weeks previously in respect of a court appearance that Stephen Brown (Stanley and Sarah's youngest son) was due to make. Mr Davies was off sick and remained so until the 3rd May and Mr Pickstock was therefore asked to update the report. Mr Pickstock's addendum stated that he endorsed Mr Davies' report and supported his recommendation. Mr Davies' report had stated that:

> 'Mrs Brown presents as a capable housekeeper and mother, she is deeply fond of all her children . . . Mr Brown seems a firm but fair father to his children, he has well defined ideas on their upbringing and expects obedience from them at all times . . . . In the main relations in the family group appear to be very good. There is frequent contact between those members who live away from home and the remainder of the family.'

Mr Pickstock completed his addendum on the 24th March; it is thus documented that on that date he felt that the Browns were providing an adequate home.

116. **Mr Pickstock's next visit was on the 26th March** when he noted that Paul and Liam were well and happy and that Pauline had not visited. As previously agreed between Mr Pickstock and Mrs Costello the Place of Safety Order was allowed to lapse. The file was not read—since it was lost until May 1976—and no contact was made with Mr Wylde. We find, despite certain documentary evidence to the contrary (see paras 185 and 215), that no visit to Grasswood Road was made in April or May 1976.

117. **In April 1976 Mrs Penk, Specialist Officer Child Care in the Social Services Department, commenced a review of the At risk Register.** She found that the Register had been used not just for non-accidental injury cases but also for children 'at risk' of certain medical conditions. There was very little information on why children had been placed on the Register and so she decided to work methodically through the cases in alphabetical order. The object was to consider in each case whether or not the child needed to remain on the Register. This exercise proved to be a mammoth task which threw up several inadequacies in the system, eg. children had changed addresses and this was not recorded; some agencies were unaware of children placed on the Register by their own staff. The task of reviewing the names became a detective exercise of large proportions at a time when Mrs Penk had no clerical support.

118. On the 21st April Mrs Penk reached the names of Paul and Liam and wrote to Mr Wylde asking him to review them, Mr Wylde wrote back on the 29th April, returning the review form (which remained in Mrs Penk's file until she discovered it there on the 12th August 1976) and saying that the case had been transferred to Central Wirral. Unfortunately Mrs Penk took no further action on the case because of pressure of work; at this time she was heavily involved in a campaign to recruit foster parents. Appropriate action would have alerted Central Wirral to the fact that Paul and Liam were on the At Risk Register and this should have resulted in a review of the case and a full search for the file. We recognise that Central Wirral might not have taken any action because:

a. the children had been placed on the Register when they were living with Pauline and since she had now departed the reason for Registration could be said to have been removed; and

b. Mr Pickstock and Mrs Costello saw no particular problems in the case at that time.

Nevertheless when Mrs Doran rang on the 22nd June 1976 (see para 125) Mr Pickstock would have been more alert to the possibility of child abuse.

119. On the 6th May, two months after **Mrs Sayer** had spoken to six social workers at Birkenhead in an attempt to discover Paul and Liam's address, a social worker from Birkenhead rang her to say that the family had transferred to Central Wirral. On the 10th May she found out from Central Wirral that Mr Pickstock was the Social Worker in charge of the case. On the 13th May he telephoned her and reassured her that all was well, but at that time he did not have the Browns' full address on him and promised to ring back with the details. Mrs Sayer then went off sick for several months and therefore Mr Pickstock did not pass on the address.

120. On the 1st March 1976 Paul and Liam were registered with **Dr Vaughan Roberts,** a GP who lives and practises on the Woodchurch Estate. He had been Stanley and Sarah's GP since March 1969. Both Stanley and Sarah and all the Browns who live on the estate are still his patients. Since 1970 Dr Vaughan Roberts has been in single-handed practice and in 1976 had 3,000 patients on his list. He told us that he does not operate an appointments system and patients attend surgery whenever they wish. By March 1976 he had visited 43 Grasswood Road no more than twice but Stanley and Sarah frequently went to the surgery.

121. **On the 14th June Stanley took Liam to see Dr Vaughan Roberts complaining that he was sleepy and unsteady on his legs.** Dr Vaughan Roberts referred Liam to **Dr Vernon Jones, Consultant Paediatrician at Birkenhead Children's Hospital.** Dr Vaughan Roberts, in his referral letter to Dr Vernon Jones, stated that Liam, aged 3 years was:

> 'not progressing well, poor eater, very sleepy all the time, unsteady on his legs, walks as if drunk'.

Most of the information in this letter was probably obtained from Stanley in the surgery. Dr Vaughan Roberts had known the Brown family for many years and had prescribed medicines for depression for both Stanley and Sarah.

He also knew that Paul and Liam had only recently arrived with the Browns. If Dr Vernon Jones had had this crucial information, that the boys had been well when they arrived with the Browns only four months previously, it would have alerted him to the fact that the history he was given was false.

122. In the Outpatients Department Dr Vernon Jones obtained from Sarah, who accompanied Liam, a history that was largely fabrication. She told Dr Vernon Jones that Pauline had been married to her son David but had left after a week and had been away for 5 years on the coasters, working as a stewardess, with the two children. She had returned with Paul and Liam in February 1976. At that time Liam could not walk or talk but was now beginning to do so. The impression that Dr Vernon Jones gained was that this boy had been living in a cabin on the coasters, understimulated and neglected, but that now he was with his mother's mother-in-law things were beginning to improve, This erroneous impression was compounded in the contemporary hospital outpatients notes and in Dr Vernon Jones' letter to Dr Vaughan Roberts. The truth was of course just the opposite; from April 1975 to February 1976 Paul and Liam had been with excellent foster parents and in February 1976 both looked handsome and well, both walked and talked normally for their age, and Liam was described as chubby.

123. Dr Vernon Jones examined Liam and noted his mixed parentage. He also noted the fact that he smelt of urine. His records show that he regarded Liam as a remarkably quite, docile and withdrawn boy who was not interested in his surroundings. No abnormal physical signs were noted except that his height was average and his weight below the third percentile for his age, ie. three children in every hundred of his age would weigh as little as he did. Most paediatricians would look for some explanation for such a low weight, for example small parents, very low birth weight, illness or underfeeding. With the information obtained from Sarah the explanation would be that Liam had been underfed, and had perhaps weighed even less, but was now improving. The truth is more likely to be that if he was chubby when leaving his foster parents in February 1976 he had lost 3–4 kgs by the 22nd June 1976.

124. Immediately after the outpatients clinic on the 22nd June Dr Vernon Jones wrote to Dr Vaughan Roberts relating the history he had heard from Sarah, emphasising that Liam's condition had presumably been worse and was now improving, but that nevertheless Liam was a remarkable case, rather like 'Sabu the Elephant Boy'. He told Dr Vaughan Roberts that **Mrs Doran the Hospital Senior Social Worker,** would be looking into Liam's background with the Social Services Department and that he would ask a Clinical Medical Officer, Dr Black, to test Liam's hearing and intelligence. An appointment for this test was made for the 22nd July.

125. After examining Liam Dr Vernon Jones arranged for Sarah and Liam to see Mrs Doran. Mrs Doran obtained a significantly different history from Sarah. Sarah told her that the children had been in foster care but were in such a bad state that it was agreed with Social Services that they should live with her. Mrs Doran realised that Sarah's story was unlikely to be true and she therefore contacted Mr Wylde at the Birkenhead Office. Mr Wylde

confirmed that the removal of Paul and Liam from their foster home was not effected with his approval or at his instigation and suggested that Mrs Doran should contact the Central Wirral Office who were now looking after the case. Mrs Doran then rang Central Wirral and spoke to Mr Pickstock. According to Mrs Doran Mr Pickstock was able to relate that he had been supervising the family for some months and he thought both the boys might be received into care again. He considered the grandmother coped reasonably and was well experienced in child management having reared some 18 children of her own, but he felt that to accept these two when she was well into her own middle age might well prove too heavy a burden. Mr Pickstock said he would visit and discuss the financial problem that had been mentioned. (Sarah had told Mrs Doran that she had not been getting any payment for looking after the children). Mr Pickstock checked with the Department of Health and Social Security who confirmed that they had increased Stanley's supplementary benefit in respect of the children. Mr Pickstock also agreed to contact Miss Lloyd the health visitor; he rang once or twice and failed to make contact.

126. Having collected this information Mrs Doran wrote a detailed report on the 30th June, having discussed her findings with Dr Vernon Jones. On the same day she wrote to Mr Pickstock suggesting that he might consider applying for a nursery placement, as Sarah felt both boys were showing signs of emotional and social deprivation. Mrs Doran's long and detailed report was filed in the medical notes and on her own case file. How much of its contents were discussed with Dr Vernon Jones is not clear; what is clear is that he took no action. It seems unlikely that Dr Vernon Jones was made aware of the previous good health of Liam as in the letter of the 12th August which he wrote to accompany Paul to Walton Hospital for neurosurgery the same untrue history given by Sarah is repeated.

127. Mr Walker, Principal Hospital Social Worker, asserted that it is now routine practice to circulate **hospital social workers' reports** but we doubt whether this is a generally accepted practice in the Wirral. Although Mrs Neal sent her report on Pauline to Mrs Gurny, Mrs Doran did not send her report of the 30th June 1976 on Liam to Mr Pickstock. The reports of hospital social workers and hospital liaison health visitors are prepared primarily for the medical staff so that interlinked social and medical problems can be considered together. **In our opinion such reports should normally be circulated to Social Services Area Offices and relevant health visitors.** In appropriate cases a copy of the report should be sent to the General Practitioner. We suspect that in many cases valuable information in child abuse cases lies unused in hospital files through lack of dissemination. In order to obtain the best possible service in the interest of the child and the family **it is important for there to be mutual trust between professions.** The sharing of relevant medical information which has a bearing on a patient's social behaviour or condition can be of benefit not only to the social worker but also to the doctor. The medical and social information must always be regarded as confidential and should not be passed on without the consent of the originator. **If Mrs Doran's report of the 30th June 1976 had been sent to the Central Wirral Area Office and to Dr Vaughan Roberts (who should then have passed it on to his health visitor, Miss Lloyd the Paul Brown tragedy might have been averted.**

128. As a result of Mrs Doran's telephone call Mr Pickstock attempted to visit 43 Grasswood Road on the 23rd June but did not find the Browns in; he left a card asking them to contact him. Mrs Doran says that a few days later she contacted Mr Pickstock and found out about the abortive visit and that the Browns were receiving benefit from the DHSS.

129. **On the 24th June, two days after Liam's visit to Dr Vernon Jones, Dr Vaughan Roberts was called to 43 Grasswood Road to see Stanley who had tried to commit suicide by taking an overdose of drugs.** Dr Vaughan Roberts did not see Liam on this visit (which was made in the evening) and believes that he may not have received Dr Vernon Jones' 'Sabu' letter by this date. Dr Vaughan Roberts told us that he did not show Dr Vernon Jones' letter to Miss Lloyd because the letter stated 'He (Liam) is known to the social services in Birkenhead'. Dr Vaughan Roberts must have received the letter just before or just after the the suicide attempt and should have linked the two events, passed on the information about the suicide attempt to his health visitor and to the Social Services Department and replied to Dr Vernon Jones with the information about Stanley's overdose. There is a relationship between depression and child abuse and the knowledge that an emotionally deprived child was living with a suicidal adult should have influenced Dr Vernon Jones' actions. **We consider the failure by Dr Vaughan Roberts to inform his health visitor of Dr Vernon Jones' letter, or to inform his health visitor or the Social Services Department of Stanley Brown's attempted suicide was a serious omission. Had either the health visitor or social worker been informed of the position at that time it should have precipitated immediate action.**

130. During July Dr Vaughan Roberts prescribed for both Stanley and Sarah and Mr Pickstock made a second abortive visit to Grasswood Road after being contacted by the hospital because Liam had missed his clinic appointment of the 22nd July 1976.

**The final missed opportunity**

131. It is clear that Liam's case made an impact from a medical viewpoint on Dr Vernon Jones, hence his reference to 'Sabu the Elephant Boy'. It is also clear that he was suspicious of the history given by Sarah, hence the involvement of Mrs Doran. But in spite of his suspicions, in writing to Dr Vaughan Roberts immediately after the clinic and before Mrs Doran had completed her researches Dr Vernon Jones was effectively transmitting misleading information by quoting Sarah's story as if it were correct. Had Dr Vernon Jones set in train a thorough investigation as to Liam's medical and social history, through the Liaison Health Visitor attached to the Hospital, Sarah Brown's story would very quickly have been shown to be false. If Mrs Doran had obtained a clear picture of Liam's physical condition on discharge from the foster home this too would have confirmed the falsity of the story. In the event Miss Lloyd, who was both Dr Vaughan Roberts' attached Health Visitor and Liaison Health Visitor to Birkenhead Children's Hospital did not know that Paul and Liam were on her list until the 12th August 1976 (by which time Paul and Liam had been under Dr Vaughan Roberts for 6 months) and did not see Dr Vernon Jones' letter until our Inquiry. Dr Vaughan Roberts should have discussed the case with Miss Lloyd on the 14th June 1976, before

referring Liam to Dr Vernon Jones. Miss Lloyd could then have told the GP that she had seen Liam on the 17th February 1976 when he had appeared fit and well, apart from his chin. When Dr Vaughan Roberts received the reply from Dr Vernon Jones some time after the 22nd June he should again have discussed the case with Miss Lloyd and told her that Stanley Brown had attempted to commit suicide on the 24th June 1976. Even though Dr Vernon Jones' letter contained misleading information if Miss Lloyd had seen the letter she should have visited Paul and Liam.

132. When Dr Vernon Jones saw Liam on the 22nd June he did not have to hand all the medical information which could have been made available. He had seen Liam at Thingwall Hospital at the end of March 1975 and subsequently at St Catherine's Hospital for a follow-up appointment in June 1975. **Although the records of these visits might not have affected Dr Vernon Jones' diagnosis we consider that the Area Health Authority should consider means by which consultations at different hospitals in an Area can be drawn together.** It is a well established fact that children at risk of non-accidental injury may be taken to a variety of hospitals to escape detection; we consider that it would reduce the danger of children slipping through the hospital 'net' if a central index was set up covering all hospitals concerned with children within the Wirral. It would then be possible for hospital clerks to make a routine check of the index on all new patients, without having to rely on the possibly untruthful history given by the parent. We understand that the records for St Catherine's, Thingwall and Birkenhead Children's Hospitals are already stored at St Catherine's; this could provide the basis for an experimental scheme covering Birkenhead.

133. The events of the 22nd June provide another occasion when if different actions had been taken the tragedy might have been averted. Had Dr Vernon Jones received and considered all the information that was available to the GP, the health visitor and the Hospital Senior Social Worker he would have realised the vital fact that Liam was normal in size and development in February 1976. Having realised this he should have admitted Liam, watched his weight increase rapidly in hospital and his demeanour change equally rapidly. **If he had had this information he should have called a case conference.** At the case conference Dr Vaughan Roberts would have been able to refer to Stanley's suicide attempt and to describe the extended Brown family, and the Central Wirral social workers would have been able to provide information from their files to support the case for removing the children from the Browns.

**The Brown family**

134. Stanley Brown, (David's father) is registered disabled because of a wasting disease in one leg and is short sighted, (seven of his nine children suffer from varying degrees of progressive familial myopia). Stanley has been unemployed since 1958. His wife Sarah Brown is also registered disabled because of arthritis and obesity. Of their nine living children, one is blind and partially-hearing, four are partially-sighted (including one who was classified as educationally subnormal at school) and two are short-sighted. The Social Services Department's numerous files on the extended family paint an inconsistent picture of a problem family. The following quotes, gleaned

from the 12 files on the family which we saw, may give some idea of the confused picture which the Browns would have presented to the Central Wirral Office, if anyone had read the files:

1961 'During 1961 P and 2 of his brothers spent 6 weeks at a convalescent home because of malnutrition'.

1965 'Home conditions—dreadful . . . very little cleaning ever done'.

1965 'Mr Brown is intolerant of his family and it takes little to provoke him to violence'.

'Mrs Brown is protective towards all the children and usually complains to the NSPCC Inspector and other officials when her husband becomes aggressive'.

1965 Welfare Officer unable to support P's application for a guide dog: 'This family is also well known to social workers as a problem family'.

1969 'Since moving to Woodchurch she (Sarah) seems to keep the house reasonably clean'.

12.10.73 Memo from Miss Lloyd to Social Services Department about baby(A-M) daughter of David Brown and ND living at 43 Grasswood Road:

'This family background is very unstable. From the point of view of the baby's total health and welfare would be grateful for further investigation to be undertaken. There is no actual evidence that the child is neglected but perhaps this report will outline the cause for concern . . . . The Brown family appear to be the more stable (ie than A-M's maternal grandparents) . . . . My own observation of the Brown household does not give cause for concern.'

(Later, undated, social report on A-M says: 'from approximately August to November 1973 the mother and the child were living in the putative father's home with his family and it was during this period that suspicion arose regarding possible NAI[1] to A-M').

11.3.74 F alleges that Stanley tried to kill him with a belt. Sarah says for years Stanley has knocked her about and despite many an argument he was still picking on the children. Stanley is described as 'an inadequate man who has not worked for years and is afraid of anyone in authority.' The social worker records 'I think that it is important that supervision be maintained in view of the fact that he *may* become more agressive as he becomes older and she (Sarah) may be less capable of taking it as she becomes older'.

28.6.74 Request from F to be placed as a lodger with Mrs V because of breakdown in the home situation.

27.10.75 J concerned that his brother S is being victimised by Stanley and Sarah.

20.1.76 Allegation that J's wife is neglecting their 6 week old baby and using 'considerable force' on the baby.

135. In 1976 Stanley and Sarah were living in a Council house on the Woodchurch Estate. This large estate is made up of pleasant terraced houses

[1] NAI=Non-Accidental Injury

and bleak tower blocks. At the fringes of the estate the houses are neat and well kept but the centre around the tower blocks is an area of multiple deprivation. Many of the families in this central area are known to the Social Services Department. The Brown's home, 43 Grasswood Road, is a terraced house a stone's throw from one of the tower blocks, Fernybrow Gardens. The Woodchurch Estate has a Tenants' Association whose Public Relations Officer came forward to give evidence to us about the attitude of the staff and members of Wirral Borough Council towards the residents of the Estate. We are grateful for this assistance from the Association.

**Disclosure of addresses of children in care**

136. A difference of view and practice emerged during the evidence to our Inquiry as to whether or not the addresses of children in care should be given to parents and relations. In our opinion this is a matter which cannot be the subject of any finite rule or practice. In each case it must be a question of judgement by the Social Worker, in consultation with his Seniors. In many cases there is a real hope that the child will be restored sooner or later to family life and normally only good can come from a child retaining contact with his family. In many cases foster parents have been extremely helpful in reuniting families. In exceptional cases a child or parent may be so disturbed that contact would be harmful; in such cases the address would have to be withheld temporarily or permanently. In all cases the foster parents' consent is required before their address is divulged.

137. As a separate issue it was suggested to us that some social workers, as a matter of policy, refused to disclose to health visitors the addresses of children in care. The problem that some health visitors were finding in obtaining addresses from certain social workers was brought to the attention of Mrs Riley, their Nursing Officer, who told us that she had received a significant number of such complaints. Mrs Riley had referred the problem to Miss Rowlands, the Divisional Nursing Officer (Community), and on the 19th March 1976 a meeting was held at Central Wirral Area Office with both Miss Rowlands and Mrs Riley present at which the problem was discussed. As a result of this meeting the feedback of information from the Social Services Department to health visitors gradually improved. The present policy is that health visitors are routinely advised of changes of address via the Movement Notice system. **We consider that good communication between health visitors and social workers is vital. Health visitors should always be informed by the Social Services Department of any change in address of children in care.**

**Health visitors and GP attachment**

138. Dr Vaughan Roberts' failure to communicate with Miss Lloyd about his correspondence with Dr Vernon Jones illustrates the value and importance of a regular communicative relationship between the General Practitioner and his health visitor. Dr Vaughan Roberts did not inform Miss Lloyd of the suicide attempt nor did he show her Dr Vernon Jones' letter concerning Liam. Dr Vaughan Roberts told us that he would not inform Miss Lloyd of young children coming on to his panel unless he was 'concerned about the patient or the family or the conditions'. Miss Lloyd now visits Dr Vaughan Roberts weekly. Dr Vaughan Roberts said that in 1976:

'She used to come once a week and I told my staff to give her every possible help. She could see what notes she wanted and she would come into me and discuss any points she had in her notebook that she was working on, and if I was worried about a case I would mention it to her'.

139. We also heard evidence from the two other General Practitioners with whom Paul and Liam had been registered on their relationships with their health visitors. **We are concerned at the lack of communication between Dr Owers and his health visitor.** When asked in what sort of circumstances he would communicate with his health visitor Dr Owers told us:

'Very rarely. I cannot recall specifically asking a health visitor to help in any case. I think occasionally a health visitor has got in touch with me about a young baby just discharged from hospital, something in that line'.

Clearly Dr Owers does not yet understand the role of the health visitor. Dr Moore told us that during the early years of GP attachment of health visitors he too was unclear about their role and function. However over the years he has developed a close working relationship with his health visitor (Mrs Sayer) and he feels that he has learned a great deal from her. He now sees health visitors as 'extremely useful and extremely knowledgeable' with:

'a great knowledge of local authority services, regular contacts with the local authority, doctors, clinics, nurses and with the Social Services; and specialised developmental knowledge, developmental milestones in children, and so on'.

Dr Moore's health visitor now sees every child on his list, and she is notified each week of any alterations to the list. **We were encouraged by the evidence of Dr Moore and we hope that other GPs will follow his example.**

140. Although we recognise that we heard evidence from only a very small sample of GPs and health visitors we were concerned about the working of health visitor attachment to GPs and we feel that the present system would benefit from closer examination at national level. The working relationship of Miss Lloyd and Dr Vaughan Roberts might be more accurately described as health visitor liaison rather than health visitor attachment. The health visitor is an independent member of the primary care team with her own particular contribution to make. Both health visitor and GP have equally important roles to play in this team and an understanding of each other's role will help them to work together as a team to the benefit of the community. **If health visitors are attached to GPs it is up to both parties to ensure that there is effective communication.** Without good communication the policy of health visitor attachment to GPs will not work.

**The transfer of files between Area Offices**

141. In 1976 there were numerous complaints about the delays in transfer of files by the courier system. There was little direct contact between the social workers involved regarding clients who had moved from one Area to another. The system has now been considerably improved and the chances

of a file becoming lost in transit should have been eliminated. When a case is transferred there is now an initial discussion between the respective Area Officers; the running record is brought up to date and future plans are described; a Movement Notice is completed (thus alerting others including health visitors and the At Risk Register team to the move); a joint visit to the home of the client by the old and new social workers from the two Area Offices is made; and the file is then transferred by hand to the new Area by the Area Officer or the Area Administrative Officer. The file is accompanied by a tear-off acknowledgment slip and each Area Office keeps a book of all files despatched and received.

## CHAPTER SEVEN

# THE 11th–17th AUGUST 1976

142. At 10 pm on **Wednesday the 11th August 1976** Sarah rang for a doctor and then an ambulance and Paul, now 4 years old, was admitted to Birkenhead Children's Hospital. Paul had become deeply comatosed, had bruises all over his legs, buttocks and back, and one bruise on his forehead. There was also bleeding into the back of his eyes, his limbs were spastic and his breathing was slow and gasping, which suggested severe brain damage. In the early hours of the Thursday morning an anaesthetist, Dr Black, was called in to resuscitate Paul and on his return home at breakfast time he mentioned to his wife that the hospital were arranging to admit 'the brother'. Dr Black was under the impression that child abuse was in everyone's minds.

143. At 8.40 am on **Thursday the 12th August** Mrs Sowery, Nursing Officer at Birkenhead Children's Hospital, telephoned Mrs Doran at her home, as Mrs Doran usually went to another hospital on Thursday mornings. Mrs Sowery asked Mrs Doran to come in to see Paul as she thought that he was a possible case of non-accidental injury. Mrs Doran and Mrs Sowery then went to see Paul and both agreed that his injuries were caused non-accidentally. Although the actions of both Mrs Doran and Mrs Sowery would seem to confirm this 'diagnosis' nowhere in the medical notes has any doctor written the words 'non-accidental injury', or 'NAI', or 'child abuse'. The houseman wrote as a diagnosis '?Trauma, ?Poisoning'. Dr Paul, the Locum Consultant Paediatrician, wrote 'probably had Encephalitis with Status Epilepticus' although commenting on Paul being malnourished with a lot of bruising and scratch marks all over the body. During the day skeletal X-rays and photographs were taken; both are usually done in cases of non-accidental injury.

144. As soon as Mrs Doran had seen Paul on the Thursday morning she telephoned the Central Wirral Office to speak to Mr Pickstock and since he was on holiday she spoke to his Senior, Mrs Costello. The details of this conversation are a major cause of disagreement. Mrs Costello later found her contemporary note of the call:

> 'Phone call from Kay Doran. Paul Brown taken to hospital last night in a collapsed condition. At present on life support system—extensive loss of weight—not expected to survive. Cause not known—bruises on legs'.

Mrs Doran, in her evidence to us, maintained that she made it clear to Mrs Costello that Paul had been non-accidentally injured. In Mrs Doran's contemporary record this first telephone call to Mrs Costello appears to be mainly concerned with finding out information about the children. As a result of the telephone call Mrs Costello and Mr Evans, the Area Officer, looked through the file and for the first time saw Mrs Heffer's letter to Mr McDermott putting the children on the At Risk Register. The effect of this discovery was to 'push the panic button' at Central Wirral. Mr Evans immediately rang Mr Pickstock at home to discover if he had known that Paul and Liam were on the Register. Mr Pickstock had no knowledge of the Registration, having put the case file away unread when he finally obtained it in May 1976.

145. During the rest of the day (the 12th August) Mrs Doran contacted numerous people including Mr Walker (her Principal Social Worker), Mrs Streatfield, Sarah Brown, Dr Vernon Jones, Miss Lloyd, St Catherine's Hospital, Mr Pickstock, Mr Wylde, and Mrs Gurny. She took out Place of Safety Orders on both boys. One reason for the Orders was to enable consent to be given for neurosurgery to be carried out in Pauline's absence. Mrs Doran's second telephone call to Mrs Costello was concerned with the need for Place of Safety Orders. Mrs Costello, apparently with the agreement of Mr Evans and Mrs Winship (Deputy Area Officer), felt that Place of Safety Orders were not necessary. Mrs Doran therefore took them out herself. The main point of disagreement stemming from the day's activities is Mrs Doran's insistence that she made it clear to Central Wirral that Paul was non-accidentally injured and therefore the Area team, who already knew the family, should take over the case. The Central Wirral Office maintain equally that Mrs Doran did not say that Paul was an NAI case and that they thought Paul was suffering from a medical condition and Liam's admission might assist in the diagnosis of Paul's illness. We consider that the truth lies somewhere between the two but that each party took up a more extreme stance than was necessary, both at the time and in the ensuing arguments. Mrs Doran felt sure that Paul had been non-accidentally injured but received no support from the two doctors who had seen him during the day—the House Officer and the Locum Consultant (Dr Paul)—and so failed to mention NAI to anyone other than Mrs Sowery in case she was wrong. Mrs Costello and the staff at Central Wirral had failed to appreciate that Paul and Liam were on the At Risk Register, had not seen them for five months, and very much wanted Paul's physical condition to be the result of a medical illness rather than non-accidental injury.

146. Meanwhile Paul's condition had deteriorated and at 5pm Mrs Sowery contacted Dr Vernon Jones who was conducting an out-patients clinic at the hospital at that time. By now the immediate need was to get Paul to the neurosurgical unit at Walton Hospital in Liverpool and this was done immediately. In his referral letter to the neurosurgeon, Mr Miles, Dr Vernon Jones made no mention of suspected child abuse but he repeated the complex background given him by Sarah Brown in June 1976 and also mentioned bruising and delay in seeking medical help. The question of when non-accidental injury was first considered to be the cause of Paul's condition and when this diagnosis was first discussed had no bearing on the management of Paul's case and whether or not he would survive. But this seemingly insignificant matter became the focus of considerable dispute at a later stage and we therefore consider the events of Thursday and Friday in some detail.

147. By the evening of the 12th August Paul had been transferred to Walton Hospital for neurosurgery. Mr Pickstock had brought Liam into hospital and Place of Safety Orders had been taken out on both boys. Mrs Doran had spoken to Mr Walker before taking out the Place of Safety Orders and later in the evening Mr Walker decided that he and Mrs Doran should see

Mr McDermott first thing the next morning to discuss the handling of the case.

148. On the 12th August after seeing Mrs Heffer's letter to Mr McDermott Mr Evans had phoned Mrs Penk to find out if Paul and Liam were still on the At Risk Register. Mrs Penk had confirmed that they were and arranged to go to Central Wirral. Arriving there at 9 am on **Friday the 13th August** she spoke to Mr Evans, Mrs Costello and Mr Pickstock. All were very concerned that the fact that Paul and Liam were on the Register had not been transmitted to Central Wirral when the case had been transferred in February/March 1976.

149. Mr Walker and Mrs Doran had meanwhile gone to see Mr McDermott to discuss Central Wirral's apparent reluctance to accept that Paul had been non-accidentally injured. Mr McDermott heard the story of the previous day's events and asked Mr Evans, Mrs Costello and Mr Pickstock to come and join the meeting. By now Mr Pickstock had gone to Walton Hospital to see the doctor about Paul and therefore Mr Evans and Mrs Costello attended without him. Mrs Doran insisted she had made it clear to Central Wirral on the Thursday that Paul was a case of NAI but Mrs Costello denied that this had been made clear to her. During the meeting with Mr McDermott Mr Pickstock was telephoned at Walton Hospital and told not to mention to the staff at the hospital that Paul and Liam were on the At Risk Register. Mr Pickstock replied that Walton Hospital were already treating Paul as a case of NAI. At one point, when Mrs Costello and Mrs Doran were away from the meeting, Mrs Costello expressed her regret at what had happened to Paul and mentioned her difficulties in supervising her team and the fear that this would be a slur on her personal career. Mrs Doran recorded this private conversation in her running record on Paul's case file and this action by Mrs Doran became a major cause of trouble at a later stage.

150. On **Monday the 16th August** Pauline visited the hospital in a very distressed state and asked Mrs Doran if the local authority could take over control of the children; after discussion with Mr Evans Mrs Doran wrote out a form to this effect which Pauline signed.

151. On **Tuesday the 17th August a case conference was held.** This case conference was chaired by Mr McDermott and was attended by Mrs Penk, Mr Wylde, Mrs Winship (in the absence of Mr Evans who was off sick and Mrs Costello who was on Holiday), Mr Pickstock, Mrs Doran, Mr Walker and the social worker from Walton Hospital; Mrs Sayer and two senior health visitors; a doctor; and representatives of the police, probation service, and Wirral Department of Administration and Legal Services. The meeting opened with Mr Pickstock reading his unfinished Social History Reports on Pauline and Paul and Liam which he expanded on verbally. The meeting then appears to have dissolved into unfocussed discussion and questions. Mrs Doran read her report and the discussion and questions continued. The so-called minutes of this case conference were not so much minutes as haphazard verbatim notes. No coherent picture of the discussion or conclusions of the case conference emerges from these notes. They do however suggest that the case conference was not well chaired and that the discussion was allowed to ramble.

The conclusions of the meeting appear to be that:

a. further consideration is required;

b. the police should continue their enquiries;

c. Liam should be lodged in a place of safety; and

d. care proceedings should be considered.

152. Towards the end of the meeting a note purporting to come from Dr Vernon Jones was read out. Mr O'Shea (Principal Assistant, Fieldwork) had written this note following a telephone call from a doctor. The note, which said that Dr Vernon Jones did not believe Paul to be a case of NAI and that Dr Paul would like Liam taken into care, was handed to Mr McDermott who read it out at the case conference. Dr Vernon Jones, who only found out about this note at our Inquiry nearly 4 years later, strongly denies that he ever said that Paul was *not* an NAI case or that he could have given anyone that impression. We have no doubt that Mr O'Shea was given erroneous information by a doctor, probably Dr Paul's Registrar, concerning Dr Vernon Jones' view of the case. We are satisfied that Dr Vernon Jones did not hold such a view or instruct anyone to pass on such a view. Mr Miles, the neurosurgeon, made it quite clear that he considered that Paul's injuries were as a result of 'battering'.

**Diagnosis of child abuse**

153. When Paul was admitted to Birkenhead Children's Hospital his condition was such that the diagnosis of NAI was essentially a medical matter. We find that it was Mrs Doran and Mrs Sowery rather than the Locum Consultant Paediatrician and Senior House Officer who made the diagnosis of non-accidental injury and in the absence of support from their medical colleagues took the necessary action.

154. In this report we have frequently used the term non-accidental injury (NAI) since that was the description in use in Wirral in 1976. The term 'child abuse' is however a preferable description of the syndrome since it does not limit the problem to cases of physical injury. The spectrum of child abuse is wide and the limits are hard to define. It ranges from physical ill-treatment which may result in injury or even death, to emotional cruelty including a failure to provide love and affection, and malnutrition. Although child abuse has been recognised in this country for 20 years it is still often missed as a diagnosis because relatively few doctors see a case during their professional careers. Those who do see abused children tend for obvious reasons to be paediatricians, orthopaedic surgeons with a paediatric case load, and neurosurgeons. The importance of diagnosing child abuse in Casualty (Accident and Emergency) Departments was raised in evidence before us with the Nursing Officer at Birkenhead Children's Hospital. The diagnosis is most often made by very experienced nursing staff. The importance of paediatric training can be illustrated by the bruises on Paul's back. A paediatrically trained doctor would know that such bruises are often associated with a subdural haematoma caused by the child being picked up and shaken. A new hospital is shortly to be opened in the Wirral, at Arrowe Park. **Bearing in mind the importance of diagnosing child abuse in its widest aspects in Casualty Departments we recom-**

**mend that paediatrically trained medical and nursing staff should be available in the Casualty Department of this new hospital, and in hospitals throughout the country.**

**Wirral Area Review Committee**

155. The conduct of case conferences in the Wirral is governed by the policies of the Area Review Committee (ARC). The Wirral ARC first met in July 1974 following the DHSS Circular LASSL(74)13 of April 1974 which asked Area Health Authorities and Social Services Departments to combine to set up ARCs. There have been 28 meetings of the main Wirral Area Review Committee in the last six years and more than 28 meetings of the Monitoring Subcommittee. Representation on the Committee is wide and chairmanship has alternated between the Area Health Authority and the Social Services Department. The ARC has been influential within the Wirral and has produced three editions of a booklet on Non-Accidental Injury Alerting Procedures, each edition being revised every 2 years. All the major issues in the DHSS circular have been discussed. Many of the problems which we have mentioned, including accommodation, training, the replacement of seconded social workers, and General Practitioner involvement in NAI, have been considered. Discussions at the ARC on previous inquiries into the case of Paul Brown have been wide ranging and constructive.

**Case conferences**

156. The Alerting Procedures booklet which was current in 1975/6 states that as soon as non-accidental injury is suspected a form should be filled in; Mr McDermott Assistant Director (Fieldwork) would then convene a case conference if requested to do so on the form. No case conference was held on this family until after the 12th August 1976. **We consider that there should have been a case conference in March 1975 when Mrs Heffer wrote to Mr McDermott asking him to put the two children on the At Risk Register,** but Mrs Heffer did not use the correct form and no request to convene a case conference was made. **A case conference before allowing the Place of Safety Orders to lapse in March 1976 might well have pulled together enough information about the extended Brown family to increase the frequency of visiting by the Social Services. But the time when a case conference would have been most informative was after the visit of Liam to Dr Vernon Jones on the 22nd June 1976.** In evidence to us Dr Vernon Jones admitted that had information as to the previous good health of the children been available in June very different decisions might have been taken.

157. Dr Vernon Jones is a very experienced Paediatrician who has played a major role in the Wirral Area Review Committee. Although he attends many case conferences on his own patients he admits to finding that they are frequently rather unprofitable. This is a feeling shared by many people around the country and because of this we sought the opinions of several witnesses on the subject. Some worries were identified, the major one being the time taken up by case conferences. It takes a great deal of time to organise 6 or 7 busy people to meet at a mutually convenient hour and only too often the case conference goes on for far too long with no clear direction. Sometimes no clear decisions are reached. Since conferences are often convened at short

notice those who attend may not be adequately prepared so that discussions may become rambling and undirected. The chairing of conferences was seen by witnesses as crucial. It was felt that the chairman's responsibility was to extract information rapidly from those possessing it, to ensure that the opinions of more junior people were not ignored, and then to draw together the strands of information in order to reach some clear decisions. Some decisions that have to be reached in a case conference are: Should the child be put on the At Risk Register? Should the parents be told? Are juvenile court proceedings required. Is prosecution by the police required? Who will be the key worker? What are future plans? Some witnesses feared that if case conferences become too frequent they could lose their value; this fear may well be justified.

158. **GPs have a positive contribution to make to case conferences from their knowledge of the child and his family. Attendance at case conferences will increase a GP's understanding of child abuse and will make him more alert to spotting incipient child abuse in his practice. In the Wirral very few GPs attend case conferences; we deplore this fact.** The GPs whom we heard admitted that their knowledge of child abuse was very limited. Dr Owers told us that as far as he could recollect he had never come across a child with signs of possible non-accidental injury; Dr Moore said that he had come across three cases of child abuse in the last three years.

159. In the last four years Wirral has dramatically improved its arrangements for case conferences. Various guidelines and check-lists have been produced. All case conferences are attended by the child abuse specialist, Mr Matthews, and he circulates abbreviated minutes to all who attend. All case conferences are chaired by Area Officers of the Social Services Department who have now developed some skill at chairmanship. **We hope that the value of case conferences will be recognised as they become more efficient and decisive. The exchange of information at case conferences should remain highly confidential and each agency should retain its autonomy: the case conference should be a means of sharing responsibility and information but must not become a substitute for individual responsibility and decision making.**

## CHAPTER EIGHT

# FROM THE CASE CONFERENCE TO THE SOCIAL SERVICES COMMITTEE MEETING OF THE 19th OCTOBER 1977

### Activity after the case conference

160. After the case conference of the 17th August 1976 there were three main areas of activity in the case of Paul Brown.

a. The police were engaged in collecting the evidence which led to the prosecution of Stanley and Sarah, who were charged on the 25th August with assault. They were remanded on bail on the 20th September.

b. The Central Wirral Area Office, and Mr Pickstock in particular, were preparing the Department's case in the care proceedings in respect of Paul and Liam. This involved Mr Pickstock examining in detail the many files relating to the extended Brown family and preparing a summary of their contents, a task which he had begun before the case conference but probably only finished in September. On the 29th September care orders were made in respect of Paul and Liam. Paul remained critically ill in hospital. Liam went to live with foster parents.

c. Mrs Penk, as the Specialist Child Care Officer, was selected to write a report on the Department's handling of the case of Paul and Liam. This report is dated the 20th August. Examination of the report shows that its contents come from three main sources: the case file as it was at that time, information gleaned from the case conference on the 17th August, and oral information from Mr Pickstock. No information was obtained from his Senior, Mrs Costello, as she was away on leave. We analyse later the state of the case file at this period.

### The report of the 20th August 1976

161. In her report Mrs Penk reached the following conclusion:

'There appear to be serious faults in the communication system, which rests on a combination of formal and informal arrangements—both administratively and by direct personal contact.

We must recognise the difficulties Area staff labour under, which will affect the quality of recording and it may not be surprising that messages or reports are not recorded. However, the transmission of information and quality of recording appear to have fallen below what one would expect.'

162. The report highlighted the following failures:

a. Non-compliance with the Boarding-Out Regulations while Paul and Liam were being fostered by Mr and Mrs Shackleton.

b. Mrs Sayer's inability to obtain Paul and Liam's address from the Birkenhead Area Office.

c. When Mr Pickstock eventually obtained the case file from the Birkenhead Area Office it was put away unread.

d. Communication between Dr Vernon Jones, Mrs Doran, Dr Vaughan Roberts, Miss Lloyd and the Central Wirral Area Office was inadequate.

e. There was no proper transfer of the case and the file from the Birkenhead Area Office to Central Wirral.

163. We find that on the 20th August 1976 the running record on the case file ended with Mrs Thornton's entry dated the 20th February 1976; there were no entries by Mr Pickstock relating to the period when the case was the responsibility of Central Wirral. Before preparing her report Mrs Penk did not see any document containing the details of Mr Pickstock's visits to 43 Grasswood Road on the 5th, 9th, 19th and 26th March 1976. Mr Pickstock had prepared a running record covering the visits of March 1976. This record had been typed and a carbon copy placed on the 'day file'—a chronological file of all the typing done in the Area Office. The carbon copy records all 4 visits by Mr Pickstock and ends with the entry for the 26th March. This carbon copy did not come to light until the Heald Inquiry in July 1978. Two passages in Mrs Penk's report convince us that she did not see any documentary evidence of any visits by Mr Pickstock other than Mr Pickstock's Social History Report for the case conference (which refers to only one visit—that of the 5th March 1976):

a. 'Social Worker visited once or twice and allowed the place of safety orders to lapse—accepting the Area Officer's assessment of the case. He did not feel it necessary to continue supervision of the children since the risk element was removed when Mrs Brown moved to London'.

b. 'There was nothing in the case paper to indicate her (Mrs Doran's) referral had been followed up, although it later transpired Social Worker had made two abortive visits and planned another visit after returning from leave'.

Probably Mr Pickstock himself had forgotten about the typed running record of the March 1976 visits because his statement to the police dated the 26th August 1976 contains similar information about visiting but is as vague about dates as Mrs Penk's report. The top copy of the typed March 1976 running record was probably lying forgotten in a drawer in Mr Pickstock's desk at Central Wirral at this time.

164. In her report Mrs Penk noted that Mrs Heffer "referred the children to the At Risk Register by letter but failed to follow it up with a completed referral form and report'. Mrs Penk thereby impliedly criticised Mrs Heffer, an unqualified Social Worker who had left the Department over a year earlier. Mrs Penk omitted to state that Mrs Heffer's referral letter was specifically addressed to and dealt with by Mr McDermott. She also omitted to state that she and Mr Wylde had been in correspondence about reviewing the case of Paul and Liam and had known in April 1976 that they were on the At Risk Register and that the case had been transferred to Central Wirral. In our opinion these omissions were deliberate. This view is consistent with the omission of any mention of the matter from the Department's detailed minutes of the case conference of the 17th August. The Social History Report by Mr Pickstock circulated at that case conference merely recorded:

'24th March 1975 Request made for children to be placed on At Risk Register'.

165. Mr McDermott circulated copies of Mrs Penk's report to Area Officers and others, including Mr Douglas Jones, together with a memorandum dated the 20th August in which he stated that the purpose of the report's circulation was:

> 'to prompt an immediate review of office procedures and communication arrangements within and without the office and department, and especially with those operating in the relevant spheres of health, hospital and probation services'.

We commend the general tone of Mrs Penk's report and Mr McDermott's reaction to it. In his memorandum Mr McDermott also gave notice of a meeting to be held on the 8th September between Area Officers and Health Liaison and Senior Health Visitor staff to consider Mrs Penk's report. Minutes of the meeting of the 8th September show that all the main deficiencies and difficulties in communication brought to light as the result of the Paul Brown case were discussed: the notification to health visitors of the movement of children in care, a long standing problem in the Wirral; the failure of general practitioners to share information with health visitors and social workers, another intractable problem; the inadequacy of recording in case files with the related problems of inter-disciplinary communication and confidentiality; and referrals to the At Risk Register and the obsolete nature of the existing Register which contained names of children not thought to be at risk of NAI. In our opinion the Social Services Department and the Area Health Authority were taking a positive and constructive line on the lessons to be learnt from the Paul Brown tragedy.

**The dispute between Central Wirral and Mrs Doran**

166. On the 26th October 1976, at a meeting chaired by Mr McDermott, the first rumblings of dissent within the Social Services Department were heard. The meeting was attended by Mr Evans, Mr Pickstock, Mrs Doran and Mr Walker. A discussion ensued as to the degree of urgency with which Mrs Doran had conveyed on the telephone to Mr Pickstock on the 22nd June 1976 the suggestion that nursery placements should be found for Paul and Liam. As this conversation had occurred some four months earlier it is very unlikely that either Mrs Doran or Mr Pickstock could even then have remembered wholly accurately the tone and details of that conversation.

167. The tragedy is, and tragedy is not too strong a word for it, that this discussion was no longer of any practical importance. It is a great pity that at this early stage Mr McDermott did not impose his authority by saying that it mattered not what the details of the conversation were and that the Department would concern itself with the past only in order to draw lessons for the future. Instead this discussion became the forerunner of many discussions about minutiae which often degenerated into heated disputes among the staff of the Department in the months ahead. Meetings were attended by many people and involved senior members of the Department from Mr Douglas Jones downwards. Discussion became rancour; minutes and notes were taken; hours of scarce social worker time were wasted. By the time

of our Inquiry the battle lines had hardened amd many hours of evidence before us were devoted to a vain attempt to prove who had said what to whom and why. In our opinion the senior management of the Department must take responsibility for this waste of time and money. Mr Douglas Jones should have applied common sense and put a stop to it as soon as he heard about it; instead he took part in the discussions. These discussions, which to an outsider seem profitless and unnecessarily acrimonious, developed for a variety of reasons.

**The social worker**

168. In comparison with medicine, the law, education, nursing or accountancy, social work is a new profession. The social worker is still to some extent defining his role and the public has only the haziest of ideas of what he actually *does*. Professions acquire status in a variety of ways and having done so this status is proclaimed through a variety of 'signs': a uniform, a large office, a quiet consulting room, a large number of deferential subordinates, a large salary. The social worker has none of these and indeed would not welcome any status symbol which placed a barrier between him and his clients. Social work involves helping people with problems, often the least attractive members of society whom other agencies have given up as impossible to help. It does not mean 'curing' one client and passing on to the next, but rather working month after month, perhaps for years, with the same difficult clients. Social workers are self-critical, questioning their own performance in order to learn lessons from the handling of their own and others' cases. This sort of self-examination may make social workers appear to be obsessively inward looking. We think there is a need for much greater understanding by the public at large of social work and what it involves.

169. There is however a danger that too much critical examination of work can result in a lack of confidence by the social worker in his own judgment. Once this lack of confidence takes root the social worker is unwilling to act or to express his view for fear of being seen to make a mistake and is quick to take offence when criticised from outside. We can understand how this defensive attitude has developed and we do not believe it has been helped by previous inquiries into NAI cases in which the minute examination of errors of judgement and minor mistakes has implicity laid the blame for the tragedy on named social workers, often of very junior rank. **It is our view that the elected members of Social Services Committees and the senior management of Social Services Departments must make it plain to the social work staff that they are professional people doing a vital job and that when tragedies do occur—as they inevitably will—staff will be supported and encouraged to draw positive conclusions rather than castigated and disciplined.** With confidence in themselves and the knowledge of this support behind them social workers can perform their professional task better and their senior managers can play a more equal role in the business of running the local authority.

170. Of the 31 social workers who gave evidence to us there were a small number whose confidence in themselves had become undermined by the atmosphere of mistrust which had built up within the Social Services Department over a period of years. We have devoted some space to the characters

of some of the people involved to show how personality differences in some cases heightened existing tensions.

171. In 1976 **Mrs Doran** was a Senior, but unqualified, Hospital Social Worker of several years experience. In the past the medical social worker was the employee of the National Health Service; she was the descendant of the almoner; she mixed with the ward sisters and accompanied the consultant on his rounds; when her employer changed to the Social Services Department of the local authority she became a member of the Social Services staff and owed loyalty to the Department and its Director but much of her traditional personal service to hospital medical staff continued. In 1976, in our opinion, the differences in background and loyalties between the hospital social worker and the field social worker explain to some extent how Mrs Doran found herself warring against the contentions of the field social workers of Central Wirral.

172. We have no doubt that as a hospital social worker Mrs Doran was competent. She was certainly regarded as such by all with whom she worked. Evidence of this can be seen in her promotion, by Mr Douglas Jones, to Principal Hospital Social Worker in succession to Mr Walker in 1977. Her promotion was initially blocked by a group of Senior Social Workers, mainly from the Central Wirral Area Office, on grounds which they stressed were not personal but purely professional. They threatened to boycott her because she did not have the requisite professional qualification. Not until the post had been readvertised did she finally achieve substantive promotion. Her blacking, albeit abortive, could have done nothing to lessen her feeling of antagonism towards Central Wirral. In our opinion this action by certain social workers was unjustified. We can understand the attitude of a new profession wishing all its members to become professionally qualified and we hope that this desirable objective will soon be attained. In the meantime competent unqualified social workers with long service with an authority should be given priority for training, and promotion should be based on merit and suitability.

173. Mrs Doran's personality was a factor which contributed to the feuding. She was concerned about her own image as is revealed in the mirror-like quality and detail of her recording, including her references to the impression she made on others. Truthful and accurate though we found most of her evidence it was subjectively given. Much that she found important we found trivial. We think that, subconsciously at least and in reality unfairly to herself, she felt some responsibility for Paul's tragedy. Perhaps she felt that if only she had been more forceful and direct with Mr Pickstock and if only she herself had communicated with Miss Lloyd the tragedy would never have occurred.

174. On the other side was the Central Wirral Area Office with **Mr Evans** in charge. During 1976 Mr Evans felt himself threatened. The Chairman of the Social Services Committee, Councillor Roberts, was the member for a Ward which included densely populated housing estates within the Central Wirral Area. Councillor Roberts was an aggressive and interfering Chairman. As the local Ward Member he received many applications from people seeking

help from Social Services. Councillor Roberts expected action sharpish and if it was not forthcoming with the speed that he expected the Department, from Mr Douglas Jones downwards, felt the lash of his disfavour. Regrettably Mr Douglas Jones did not bear the brunt himself but passed it down the line. A rebuke from Councillor Roberts to Mr Douglas Jones on occasion became a rebuke from Mr Douglas Jones to a subordinate. These Councillor referrals placed great strain on the Social Services Department, particularly in Central Wirral. On one occasion Mr Evans, on sending a report to Mr Douglas Jones on a referral from Councillor Roberts, added a rider that Councillor referrals would not be dealt with more speedily than other referrals. Accidentally this rider was read by Councillor Roberts. This resulted in a rebuke to Mr Douglas Jones followed by a rebuke from Mr Douglas Jones to Mr Evans. In our opinion Mr Evans' policy expressed in his rider was correct. It is a measure of Mr Douglas Jones' own lack of confidence and reaction to criticism that he failed to make clear to Councillor Roberts and to all Councillors that their referrals could have no special priority.

175. This incident is symptomatic of Mr Douglas Jones' and his management's attitude when they themselves were subjected to outside criticism. During 1976 and 1977 Mr Evans received two oral warnings and one written warning emanating from Mr Douglas Jones under the disciplinary procedures about matters which required guidance and support rather than disciplinary action. Mr Evans told us that at one stage he and his wife had serious discussions about what they would do if he had to find alternative employment. We found no evidence of misdemeanours on the part of Mr Evans sufficient to warrant the action which was taken against him.

176. A memorandum dated the 20th December 1976 sent by Mr McDermott, on Mr Douglas Jones' instructions, to Mr Evans stated:

> 'I was directed to issue an emphatic warning that should you engage in any further action which was subsequently deemed a breach of professional conduct then this would result in the day to day management of the affairs of the Area Office passing to me'.

In our view this letter is an example of the lack of wise leadership by Mr Douglas Jones which contributed to a justified feeling among the staff at Central Wirral that they were not receiving the support from management that they deserved. The resulting low morale and lack of confidence contributed to the defensive posture of the Central Wirral Office to criticism in relation to the Paul Brown case.

177. **Mr Pickstock,** the social worker responsible for Paul and Liam from March to August 1976, was himself under great strain during 1976. We have come to the conclusion that Mr Pickstock did have some underlying personal problems. He was not a particularly effective social worker: his distaste and inaptitude for much routine work, including paper work, was compensated by an inappropriate eagerness to go out of the office on errands which gave him a sense of importance.

178. On the 20th December 1976 Mrs Costello sent a confidential memorandum to management giving a brief outline of the areas of concern that

she had had over Mr Pickstock during the previous 10 months. In order to dispel the scurrilous and unfair rumours about Mr Pickstock that were rampant in the Wirral we consider it our duty to quote verbatim from this memorandum. We are satisfied that Mrs Costello's comments were fair and accurate made as his Senior Social Worker without exaggeration or underestimation:

'*Recording* Never done unless I exert a huge amount of pressure, having to become unpleasant and insistent. It can take several weeks to get one piece of work written'.

'*Court Reports* Almost always ready for Court, however, they are rarely presented to typist in reasonable time. This causes a great deal of ill feeling within the team'.

In fairness to Mr Pickstock we should point out that he had an excessively heavy load of Court Reports to furnish in June and July 1976.

'*Drinking* Was brought to his attention by me in late February and throughout the Spring. The problem appeared to have almost disappeared until about October'.

'I understand that he has told members of the team that concern over the current situation' (ie the Paul Brown case) 'is causing him to drink more. It should be noted, however, that although I have often been able to smell alcohol on him I have never seen him affected by it'.

179. We feel that from the date of Paul's admission to hospital Mr Pickstock, like Mrs Doran, felt a sense of personal responsibility. He had failed to see the children after March 1976; he must have felt that if only he had been more persistent in his calls at 43 Grasswood Road the tragedy might have been averted. In our opinion this may explain his return to drinking in October 1976 and his subsequent nervous debility.

180. In the House of Commons on the 30th November 1979 Mr Frank Field, MP said:

'Immensely serious charges are now being made locally that the reason why the key document was missing and not submitted to the Oakes inquiry was that a person was asked not to submit the document, and in return any disciplinary action for drunkenness would not be taken against that person'.

**No evidence has been given to us to support this allegation.** Having observed Mr Pickstock, Mrs Costello and all their superiors and judged their evidence at length **we find that the allegation is without foundation.**

181. In December 1979 a Mrs Anders, a resident of Fernybrow Gardens on the Woodchurch Estate, made a statement to Councillor Wells, the Mayor of the Wirral, alleging that a social worker had been having a very squalid adulterous affair with a friend of hers in about 1976. After the beginning of our Inquiry Mrs Anders named the social worker as Mr Pickstock. This allegation became public knowledge and Mrs Anders gave evidence to us stating that the adultery had taken place before her eyes. Mr Pickstock denied the allegation and we believe him. Mrs Anders and her family have been well known to the Social Services Department for years. She has a long history

of mental instability and is given to making allegations for twisted motives of her own. We found her an utterly unreliable witness and unhesitatingly reject her allegation against Mr Pickstock. Mrs Anders also gave evidence to us that one evening in August 1976, a few days before Paul's admission to hospital, she saw Pauline Brown battering a child in arms in a street on the Woodchurch Estate and that she reported this incident forthwith to the Birkenhead Area Office by telephone. We heard detailed evidence as to the system then in operation at Birkenhead with regard to telephone referrals. We find that Mrs Anders made no such referral in relation to Pauline and we utterly reject Mrs Anders' evidence alleging an assault by Pauline on a child in August 1976. Pauline gave evidence to us and denied the allegations; we believe her denial.

182. We find that Mrs Costello in her memorandum of the 20th December 1976 fairly and accurately described Mr Pickstock's weaknesses as a social worker. **We should like to record our view that publicly and unfairly Mr Pickstock came to be regarded as the scapegoat for the Paul Brown affair.** We have no doubt that this unjustifiable treatment caused him and his family great distress. We note that Mr Pickstock is now employed in other work in the Social Services Department away from the stresses of work on the Woodchurch Estate.

183. **Mrs Costello** is a young and ambitious social worker. She clearly resents any criticism which she thinks may affect her reputation or career. Her reaction to criticism is indicative of a lack of confidence in herself as a Senior Social worker, as is illustrated in a memorandum dated the 5th April 1978 commenting on the Report of the Oakes Committee:

> 'With regard to the Report's comments over the lapsing of the Place of Safety Order in March 1976, I find I can only be critical and accuse them of reacting as only an uninformed member of the public would'.
>
> 'With regard to the report's comments regarding my method of supervision in this case being inappropriate, the only way for me to have avoided such comment would have been to be highly critical of Mr Pickstock. I did not feel that that was appropriate during the course of an independent inquiry. However, my position regarding this matter is entirely defensible and over the last two years has been a matter of constant discussion between myself, my senior colleagues, area officer and Assistant Director. Suffice it to say that I stopped being Mr Pickstock's supervisor, at my request, some time ago and would refuse to be responsible for him ever again'.

With their contrasting personalities Mrs Costello and Mrs Doran found themselves embattled.

### The report of the 3rd December 1976

184. On the 29th November 1976 Paul Brown died and the pressure on the Social Services Department increased. Mrs Penk prepared a report dated the 3rd December for the purpose of a meeting called by Mr Douglas Jones for the 9th December. In this report she omitted to mention the personal involvement of Mr Douglas Jones, Mr McDermott and Mr Hotchkiss in the case in March 1975, presumably because they were her superiors. In dealing

with Mr Pickstock's involvement Mrs Penk supplied additional information to her report of the 20th August stating that 'the Place of Safety Orders were allowed to lapse following discussions with' Mrs Costello, and that Mr Pickstock 'agreed with Mrs Costello that he would visit from time to time although the case was not to be part of his active caseload'. We find that Mrs Penk still had not seen any running record of Central Wirral's involvement and that this information was given to her orally by Mrs Costello who intended thereby to state her own position. The general tenor of this report was critical but balanced and is no discredit to Mrs Penk.

185. The meeting on the 9th December 1976 was chaired by Mr Douglas Jones and attended by Mrs Penk, Mrs Doran, and Mr Pickstock among many others. Its purpose was to describe in detail the personal involvement of those present in the Paul Brown case. The minutes disclose a rambling and ill-directed discussion with points of view as much as statements of fact being made. They also disclose some dissension between Mr Pickstock and Mrs Doran. Probably at this meeting Mr Douglas Jones ordered that the Central Wirral case file be brought up to date. We find that after this meeting Mr Pickstock brought the running record up to date, continuing it in manuscript on the top copy of the typed record of his March visits. We also find that the running record was in this state—part typed and part in manuscript—when seen by Mr Evans later in December. Mr Evans made out a document dated the 21st December 1976 entitled 'Recorded involvement from Central Wirral Area Office' upon which is written 'data extracted from case records'. In this record he notes 'March/June 76 2 visits (A Pickstock) 43 Grasswood Road (Brown Family)'. We find that these two visits did not in fact occur but represent what Mr Pickstock considered that he should have done. On any visits to 43 Grasswood Road after the 26th March 1976 Mr Pickstock did not see Paul and Liam.

**The meetings of January 1977**

186. On **the 17th January 1977** another meeting was held, again chaired by Mr Douglas Jones, when the dissensions between Mrs Doran and Central Wirral became more marked and acrimonious. Mr Douglas Jones began this meeting by stating his own personal involvement in the case in March 1975. The minutes record this statement from him: 'A case conference was held later in the morning of 19th and appropriate action initiated'. This was a specious gloss on what was no more than an ad hoc case discussion between himself, Mr McDermott, Mr Hotchkiss and Mrs Heffer. By October 1977 the phrase had assumed even greater dignity in a report intended to be submitted to the Social Services Committee. It became 'A case conference was convened that morning'. This is an illustration of the danger of allowing fact to become propaganda. The meeting continued unhappily. Mrs Gurny's minuted comment gives the tone: 'Took extreme exception to Mrs Streatfield's comments recorded in report'. A dispute arose in relation to the transfer of the file from Birkenhead to Central Wirral. Mr Pickstock asserted that on one occasion he had asked Mrs Gurney for the file; she could not recall this. Mrs Thornton asserted that she had prepared the file and handed it to administration indicating that the transfer was urgent. Mr Evans asserted that the first contact by Birkenhead with Central Wirral was on the 5th March 1976. Mr Douglas Jones adjourned this dispute for a further meeting.

187. The meeting, attended by 16 social workers, most of senior status, then went on to discuss Mrs Doran's involvement in the case in June and on the 12th August 1976. Dispute ranged over the telephone conversation between Mr Pickstock and Mrs Doran on the 22nd June. Again Mr Douglas Jones deferred this matter to a further meeting. A further argument arose over the propriety of taking out Place of Safety Orders on the 12th August and as to whether Dr Vernon Jones' view on the 17th August was that it was *not* a case of non-accidental injury.

188. On **the 21st January 1977** the meeting to clarify the circumstances surrounding the transfer of the file and case from Birkenhead to Central Wirral was held. Five social workers attended. The meeting reached no satisfactory conclusion. No one had examined the files of the Birkenhead Area Office and it was not until after our Inquiry was set up that a receipt for the file from Central Wirral dated the 8th March 1976 was discovered in the Birkenhead Office.

189. On **the 25th January 1977** a meeting was held to discuss the telephone conversation of the 22nd June 1976 between Mrs Doran and Mr Pickstock. Attending the meeting were Mr Evans, Mrs Winship, Mrs Costello, Mr Pickstock, Mrs Penk, Mrs Doran and Mr Walker. The meeting became very heated on the old points of the details of the telephone call, the propriety of Place of Safety Orders on the 12th August, and whether or not Mrs Doran had indicated to Mrs Costello that it was a case of NAI. In the dispute Mr Walker took Mrs Doran's side and Mrs Penk Central Wirral's. Once again there was no conclusion, indeed the dispute continued as the witnesses gave evidence before us.

190. To the outside reader these disputes may appear futile and absurd. Sadly for the participants they were important. We have given details of these disputes only to illustrate the inappropriateness of round table discussions as a fact finding forum. **One astute person could have examined all the files, interviewed all the relevant witnesses and reached the conclusion that mattered, that there had been a failure of clarity and of detail in communication. That important but old lesson could have been given without hours of wasted time and years of recrimination.**

**The report of March 1977**

191. In March 1977 a further lengthy report on the Paul Brown case was produced, this time in the form of a factual chronological account of the case rather than as a judgemental account. A copy of the report was supplied to the DHSS and a copy with names deleted was given to Councillor Roberts. There are certain omissions from this report. In our opinion these omissions were deliberate and could only have been made with the approval of the Departmental Management Team. We believe that the omissions were made in the hope that the spotlight would not fall upon senior staff of the Department and render them liable to possible criticism.

192. Nowhere in the report is there any mention of Paul and Liam being placed on the At Risk Register in March 1975 or of Central Wirral's ignorance of the Registration. The report contains this misleading statement:

'On 17.2.76 and unknown to the SW Mrs Brown removed the children from their foster home and took them to the home of Mr and Mrs Brown senior, where she and her husband were staying'.

The fact that Mrs Gurny had two telephone conversations with the Shackletons on the 17th February and told them she could do nothing to help them is not mentioned.

193. The report contains this statement for which there was no factual basis:

'April-May 1976—A visit was made each month and the situation gave no cause for concern'.

Mrs Penk's explanation for this sentence was that it was her interpretation of an entry on the running record and that Mr Evans had listed the same entry as 'March/June—2 visits' in his list of Central Wirral involvement, prepared in December 1976.

**Mrs Doran's running record**

194. At a meeting at about this time, it matters not when, but possibly on the 1st February 1977, Mrs Doran revealed a confidential remark by Mrs Costello which she had recorded in her Paul Brown case file in the entry for the 13th August 1976 as follows:

'Mrs Costello then in confidence to this file expressed regret concerning Paul's present state, stating that due to difficulties at Moreton Office supervision of her team had been virtually impossible. She had complained about this to Mr Evans. Mrs Costello clearly indicated to SSW that she felt this incident might be a slur on her personal career'.

195. Mrs Costello was furious that this private conversation had been recorded in a case file and then revealed. We consider that her fury was justified for a breach of a private, informal, confidential converstion. Mrs Costello frankly stated in evidence to us that the content of Mrs Doran's note was substantially correct. Mrs Doran's revelation was naturally very embarrassing for Mrs Costello and did nothing to improve relations between Central Wirral and Mrs Doran.

196. This dispute came before Mr Douglas Jones. Quite rightly he took the view that comments by one social worker about another social worker had no place in a case file. Mr Douglas Jones asked Mrs Doran why she had included this entry but Mrs Doran was unable to give any explanation. He therefore asked Mrs Doran to remove the offending entry. She refused, pleading that as a matter of principle she would not alter a running record. No doubt Mr Douglas Jones became angry at Mrs Doran's stubbornness as he saw it. Mrs Doran had one or two meetings with Mr Douglas Jones as well as a telephone conversation during which he tried to have the offending entry expunged. Probably Mrs Doran suspected that it was not only Mrs Costello's fury at the breach of confidentiality but also the criticism of the Central Wirral Area Office implicit in her record which made Mr Douglas Jones so keen for the entry to be expunged. In our opinion this suspicion may not have been ill-founded.

197. On the 1st March 1977 a compromise was reached, or rather a charade of one. Mrs Doran sent the originals of her running record to Mr Douglas Jones but retained photostat copies recording on them these words:

> '1.3.77 Photostat copy; Original entry sent to Director of SSD, at his request, after he had been approached by Mrs Costello. Mr J Walker, Principal Social Worker, advised SSW to send original to Director, but to make photostat to protect her professional integrity'.

This incident illustrates the degree of mutual mistrust which had developed in the Social Services Department by this time.

198. **In our opinion a case file is never the proper repository of comments, whether complimentary or critical, by one social worker upon another. If it be thought right to record such comments they should be made in a private memorandum.**

**Councillor Walker**

199. This incident had unfortunate consequences. It became the subject of gossip and no doubt its significance was magnified in the retelling. A year later the story came to the ears of Councillor Walker, a member of the Social Services Committee. On the 7th April 1978 as a subterfuge he made use of his wife, a health visitor, to telephone Mrs Doran as from one professional to another and ask her if she had been asked to change her evidence or file. According to Councillor Walker Mrs Doran replied that she would not say whether this was true or untrue. Mrs Doran told us that she admitted to Mrs Walker that pressure had been brought on her to change her files. In any event she ended the conversation when she realised that Mrs Walker was the wife of a Councillor. It is a measure of Mrs Doran's basic honesty and loyalty that she at once reported the conversation to Mr Wylde and then Mr Douglas Jones.

200. The importance of the telephone conversation between Mrs Doran and Mrs Walker is that it occurred on probably the same day that Councillor Walker received his copy of the Oakes report. This increased his scepticism as to the validity of the report and the bonafides of the Department's account of the handling of the Paul Brown case. We also consider that it substantiated in his mind the belief that the so-called 'missing memo' contained evidence damning to the Department and was deliberately suppressed.

201. Mrs Doran was also asked by Mr Douglas Jones to remove a sentence from her statement to the police signed by her on the 14th February 1977 and required for the prosecution of Stanley and Sarah. Mrs Doran refused. The sentence said that despite her (Mrs Doran's) telephone call and letter of the 22nd June 1976 to Central Wirral Area Office Sarah had not received any support from them. We are convinced that this unwise request by Mr Douglas Jones was motivated by a desire on his part that the Paul Brown case should not evoke criticism of his Department. We consider at some length the reasons for Mr Douglas Jones' fear of criticism and feeling of vulnerability at this time in Chapter Eleven.

**Mr Pickstock's running record**

202. The proceedings in the Wallasey Magistrates Court, when Stanley and Sarah were committed for trial at the Liverpool Crown Court, were heard on the 22nd and 23rd June 1977. Sometime before, and possibly in contemplation of the proceedings, Mrs Costello examined the running record which had been prepared by Mr Pickstock in December 1976 (using the top copy of the March 1976 typed running record and continuing in manuscript) and later typed. This examination of the record could well have taken place at about the same time that she discovered that Mrs Doran had entered on her case file the confidential conversation of the 13th August 1976. In our opinion the purpose of Mrs Costello's examination of Mr Pickstock's running record was proper. She was his Senior Social Worker and had a duty to supervise him. Mr Pickstock had the reputation of being a bad keeper of files and records. File keeping and running records were matters which particularly concerned Mrs Costello; she rightly held the strong view that the good social worker kept professional files and records which are part of his essential tools of trade.

203. We find that Mr Pickstock's running record as seen by Mrs Costello consisted of six typed pages. They took the history of Paul and Liam from the 5th March 1976 to the 19th October 1976. They were typed on a Central Wirral Office typewriter using a blue-black typewriter ribbon. The typist was Mrs Rainford, Mr Pickstock's usual team typist. On her examination of the running record Mrs Costello discovered certain entries which she considered to be unprofessional because they contained contentious comments relating to Mrs Doran. Probably these contentious comments related to the telephone conversation of the 22nd June 1976 between Mrs Doran and Mr Pickstock. Therefore Mrs Costello decided that these contentious comments should be excised. If Mrs Rainford had typed the part-typed part-manuscript running record as seen by Mr Evans when preparing his list in December 1976 she would have typed the entry: 'March/June 76 2 visits' onto page 1, but she may accidentally have omitted it. Such an omission is a real possibility as she was not an accurate typist; this was confirmed by the samples of her typing shown to us. An alternative is that the entry 'March/June 76 2 visits' was typed on page 1 but Mrs Costello had the entry excised because she rightly did not believe that this vague entry represented the truth and because Mr Pickstock could not substantiate the visits. Mrs Costello made two futher alterations to the text. For the entry of the 26th March 1976 relating to the Place of Safety Orders on Paul and Liam which on the carbon of the original typed running record read:

> 'Visited, children satisfactory, no knowledge of where Mrs Brown is. Decided to let order lapse, advised Mrs Costello SSW accordingly'.

Mrs Costello altered the last sentence to:

> 'Following discussion with Mrs Costello SSW it was decided to let order lapse'.

Our conclusion is that this alteration was made by Mrs Costello because from a professional point of view she was responsible for the lapsing of the Place of Safety Orders and she considered, subjectively, that the altered version represented the truth as she saw it.

204. The final alteration, on the second page of the running record, concerned what Mrs Doran told Mr Pickstock on the 12th August 1976 about Paul's admission to the Birkenhead Children's Hospital. The original version read:

> 'Discussed Paul with Mrs Doran who advised that they were concerned because there were obvious signs of neglect and malnutrition therefore they were now treating matter as suspected NAI'

During our Inquiry we discovered that the words 'therefore they were now treating matter as suspected NAI' had been covered in typists correction fluid (snopake) but were clearly visible underneath. On top of the snopake were typed the words:—'and this would not aid Paul's recovery from his head injury'. These words were deliberately used and typed in to cover the gap made by the snopaking. Mrs Costello's motive in making this alteration was twofold. Firstly she believed that the original version did not represent the truth. Secondly the original version awkwardly tended to support Mrs Doran's contention that Central Wirral were told on the 12th August 1976 that it was a case of NAI.

205. The alterations to the first page were so substantial that snopaking, as done on the second page, was not enough and the whole of the first page had to be retyped. This was done by some typist at Central Wirral other than Mrs Rainford and she used a black typewriter ribbon. She had to use a different lay-out for the text to marry up an incomplete final sentence on page 1 with its ending on page 2.

206. Our conclusions about the alterations to Mr Pickstock's running record are not made dogmatically. We heard much evidence about the alterations not all of which was consistent. Many typists gave evidence and samples of their typing were shown to us. A forensic scientist gave evidence about the examination of different typewriters, about typewriter ribbons, about typeface and the identification of typists from their typing styles. We heard at length from Mr Pickstock and Mrs Costello. The truth probably is that the alterations were made early in 1977 during the heat of the battle between Mrs Doran and Central Wirral. The alterations favoured Central Wirral's contentions with regard to such matters as the telephone conversation of the 22nd June 1976, the taking out of Place of Safety Orders on the 12th August 1976 and Central Wirral's knowledge, on that day, that the hospital were treating Paul's case as NAI. Mrs Costello was responsible for the alterations which by early 1977 she had convinced herself represented the truth. Mr Pickstock was aware of the alterations but was not responsible for them. They did not at all shed a more favourable light on his handling of the Paul and Liam Brown case. The alterations are only very marginally relevant to the question as to whether or not the Wirral Social Services Department and its staff looked after Paul and Liam with proper care. Their marginal relevance is that they throw some light on the mental attitudes of the participants. **We are satisfied that the alterations were made without the knowledge of the senior management of the Department. We are also convinced that they do not form part of any concerted wide-spread conspiracy within the Department to suppress unfavourable evidence and do not indicate the existence of any such**

**conspiracy. They are however manifestations of the lack of confidence induced by stress so prevalent throughout the Department.**

207. In the Wirral some social workers make the briefest jotting perhaps on a scrap of paper, a diary or on some existing document when seeing or immediately after seeing a client. It may be some time before they have the opportunity to transcribe the jotting into narrative form. Sometimes this transcription may be direct onto a running record, at other times it may be left for the typist to add to the running record some days or weeks later. Normally the manuscript notes will be destroyed and the social worker will not check the typed version against his original. At times during our Inquiry, often at our request, diaries, notes and documents containing notes and alterations were produced, the significance and materiality of which may not have been understood by the social workers but which assisted in our search for the truth. **We must emphasise that the sole purpose of accuracy, clarity, detail and tidiness in documentation for a social worker is to enable him to be a better social worker so far as his clients are concerned.** It would be disastrous if a social worker regarded documentation as a means of favourable presentation if he were to become subject to criticism in an Inquiry. Such an attitude could lead to specious documentation by social workers who might tend to look over their shoulders rather than positively towards their clients.

**The Magistrates Court proceedings**

208. At the Committal Proceedings on the 22nd and 23rd June 1977 Mr Pickstock gave evidence. At the conclusion of the hearing of the 22nd June Mr Pickstock was being cross-examined by Mr Kirwan, the solicitor acting for Stanley and Sarah. Mr Kirwan called for the production of the case file which on the morning of the 23rd June was brought to court by Mrs Costello. The altered version of the running record was made Exhibit No. 3 to the depositions. Before continuing his cross-examination of Mr Pickstock Mr Kirwan looked through the case file and saw a document which gossip has said was the 'missing memo'. Mr Kirwan's description of the document was vague. He did not cause it to be exhibited and he did not take a copy of it. He did not refer to it during his resumed cross-examination although a line he was adopting was the fitness of the Browns as foster parents and the responsibilities of the Social Services Department. Mr Kirwan told us that his recollection, so far as it went, was that the document was written by a woman, it was quite a small sheet of paper, and he thought related to Stanley and Sarah's fitness to act as foster parents. Our conclusion is that the document seen by Mr Kirwan was probably Mrs Doran's letter dated the 30th June 1976 to Mr Pickstock, which speaks of the difficulties experienced by Sarah with the children and the advisability of nursery placements.

209. The evidence given by Mr Pickstock at the Committal was very substantially at variance with the evidence which he gave to us and with the wealth of other oral and documentary evidence given to us. In our opinion no credence at all can be given to the evidence given by Mr Pickstock at the Committal. We have treated his evidence to us with extreme caution and looked for corroboration. At the Committal Mr Pickstock said that he saw the file in March 1976, read it and discovered that Paul and Liam were on the At Risk Register. He also conceded that Stanley and Sarah were de facto

foster parents. We do not accept that these statements represent the truth as it was in the spring of 1976. By the time of the Committal Mr Pickstock was already suffering from extreme psychological strain. Evidence to us was that he gave evidence at the Committal in a state of confusion.

**Mrs Penk's report of the 12th September 1977**

210. On the 24th August 1977 Mr McDermott sent a memorandum to Mrs Penk on the subject of the Paul Brown case. By this time public disquiet as to the Department's handling of the case was growing and Stanley and Sarah were due to appear in the Crown Court in October. In the memorandum Mr McDermott gave Mrs Penk a very proper remit. He asked for a 'simple, concise and evaluative statement' which should include:

> 'clarification of any errors or omissions which you consider serious and culpable . . . . a description of what ought to have been done—stating the legal and human obligations of this department, the AHA and any other agency . . . evidence of lessons learned and their subsequent employment within and without the department . . . '

Mrs Penk carried out this task by providing a report which was attached to a memorandum to Mr Douglas Jones dated the 12th September 1977. She performed her task, in our opinion, with a considerable degree of competence, objectivity and balance.

211. In her memorandum she stated:—

> 'I feel the case was mismanaged prior to and during the time the children were in care and that poor administration and unclear procedures influenced the continued management of the case.
>
> I feel the most serious area of administrative mismanagement was in the failure to notify the Area Health Authority of the children's movement following their discharge from care by their mother in March 1976. Whilst I do not suggest the outcome of the case hinges purely on this error, I do feel it was a significant contribution.
>
> Similarly, failure to take action prior to and during the children's period in care lost the Department the opportunity of securing the children's placement.'

In our opinion Mrs Penk's criticisms of the Department were valid and fair.

212. In the body of her report Mrs Penk commented upon: the failure to apply for assumption of Parental Rights under Section 2 of the Children Act 1948 during the spring of 1975; the failure to transfer the case and the file effectively in February 1976; the failure to notify the At Risk Register and Area Health Authority of the change of address of Paul and Liam in February 1976; Mr Pickstock's use of the Place of Safety Orders in March 1976 in relation to the suitability of the Brown's home and the long term needs of the boys; and the inadequacy of action and communication following Liam's examination by Dr Vernon Jones in June 1976. Mrs Penk's report was considered at a meeting held on the 12th September 1977 attended by Mr Douglas Jones, Mr McDermott, Mr Hotchkiss, Mr Wylde, Mrs Thornton, Mrs Costello, Mr Pickstock and Mrs Doran together with Mrs Penk herself. Another subject of discussion at this meeting was Mr Pickstock's cross-

examination, no doubt as it had been in the Magistrates Court and how it might be in the Crown Court.

**The Social Services Committee meeting of the 19th October 1977**

213. On the 11th October 1977 at the Liverpool Crown Court Stanley and Sarah Brown pleaded guilty to charges arising out of the neglect of Paul and Liam. In passing sentence Mr Justice Hollings stated:

> 'Your Counsel, Stanley Brown, has referred, very rightly, to the attitude of the Social Services. It may well be that you and your wife should not have been allowed to have the care of those children'.

The following day the Chairman of the Social Services Committee, Councillor Roberts, made a press statement in which he said that the Social Services Committee were to consider the matter on the 19th October.

214. For this meeting Mrs Penk, guided by the Department Management Team, drafted a further report. This version of the case again contained significant omissions of fact. The report contains no mention of:

a. the involvement of the Director and Mr McDermott in March 1975;

b. the inclusion of Paul and Liam on the At Risk Register on the 17th April 1975;

c. Central Wirral's ignorance of the Registration; and

d. the lack of support given to the Shackletons.

The report also contains a comment on the duty of health visitors

> 'to visit from time to time in connection with a child's health and developmental progress'

which appears to be an attempt to shift some blame for the tragedy onto the health visiting service.

215. Dealing with the period after the lapsing of the Place of Safety Orders the report states:

> 'There was no legal obligation upon the department to continue supervising the case but the Social Worker kept in touch and saw the children on 11th and 17th June when they appeared to be well'.

We find that this reference was included to add verisimilitude to the report although we consider that the draftsman must have had grave doubts whether Mr Pickstock visited and saw Paul and Liam on the 11th and the 17th June. It is possible, as Mrs Penk told us, that the explanation for the two visits, may be found in a referral form of the 9th June relating to Stephen Brown: it is possible that Mr Pickstock may have called at 43 Grasswood Road on the 11th and the 17th June to remind Stephen of his forthcoming court appearance. Mr Pickstock himself noted on the referral form that he had called at the house in error, forgetting that this (Stephen's court appearance) was not his case.

216. Mrs Penk's report concluded with the statement:

> 'Having considered the facts of the case and examined the performance of the personnel involved in its management, I am satisfied that the staff

did everything that could be reasonably expected of them in the circumstances'.

On the afternoon of the 18th October 1977, the day before the Social Services Committee meeting, Mrs Penk took a copy of the draft report to Mr Price-Jones, Deputy Director of Administration and Legal Services. Mr Price-Jones' Department is responsible for vetting all reports submitted to Committees to check that:

a. the Finance Department is aware of any financial implications;

b. the issues raised do not impinge on the responsibilities of other Chief Officers; and

c. no major policy issues are raised (these would have to be discussed among Chief Officers before submission to the relevant programme Committee and then to the Policy and Resources Committee).

The Department of Administration and Legal Services also advises on the layout and style of reports for Committees. It was suggested to us that Mr Price-Jones was the author of the conclusion quoted above; we do not believe that this was so. After reading the report Mr Price-Jones may possibly have suggested that some conclusion was required; we are satisfied that Mr Price-Jones was not the author of the conclusion although he may have suggested some of the phraseology. We are satisfied that the conclusion which appeared in the report was a conclusion which the Social Services Department Management Team intended should be put before the Committee. However we find Mr Price-Jones' conduct in relation to the whole report inexcusable. He had his own serious reservations about the validity of the report, which he knew was to be submitted to the Social Services Committee as the response to comments by a High Court Judge on the Department's handling of the case. As the Deputy Director of Administration and Legal Services he had a duty to inform the Director of Social Services of his reservations. It is no excuse for Mr Price-Jones' conduct that he may have thought that Mr Douglas Jones would not heed any adverse comments on the report. It must however be acknowledged that this was a tendentious report which should never have been submitted to the Social Services Committee and Mr Douglas Jones must accept the responsibility for this.

## CHAPTER NINE

# THE OAKES AND HEALD INQUIRIES

### The Oakes Inquiry

217. The Director's report of the 19th October 1977 was intended to exonerate the Department in its handling of Paul and Liam; its purpose was to whitewash the Department. It rightly failed in that purpose. The Social Services Committee did not accept the validity of the report's conclusion. On the day the Committee met, the DHSS wrote to the Chairman of the Area Review Committee to inform him of the Minister for Health's view that an independent inquiry should be established; the two constituent authorities of the ARC agreed to the suggestion. The inquiry, under the chairmanship of Mr J Stewart Oakes, a Recorder, was established with the following terms of reference:

'To enquire into the following matters with regard to Paul and Liam Brown during the period 1st March 1973 until 29th November 1976.

1. The services made available to the Brown family (including Mr and Mrs Stanley Brown) in respect of their care of Paul and Liam Brown.
2. The arrangements for communication between the agencies concerned in the care of Paul and Liam Brown.
3. The adequacy of the action taken to protect Paul and Liam Brown.

To submit a report and make recommendations as appropriate'.

218. The Committee heard evidence in private from the 27th February to the 2nd March and reported on the 28th March 1978. The Oakes report made the following recommendations:

'1. *Communication*

All the agencies involved should examine their system of notification in the event of the movement of children and where vital records are being transmitted both their transmission and receipt should be duly noted. Health Visitors must be informed of changes of address and changes of General Practitioner.

2. *"At Risk" Registration*

A case conference should be called in all cases referred to the "At Risk" Register. This should be convened by the Area Officer. And when a child is placed on the "At Risk" Register the file on that child should be clearly marked so that identification is obvious.

3. *Training*

Training programmes for the identification of non-accidental injury cases should be instituted as a matter of urgency.

4. *Place of Safety Orders*

Whenever a place of safety order is contemplated the Area Office should be notified and kept subsequently informed of any action or inaction.

5. *Accommodation*

That the total inadequacy of the Birkenhead office be brought to the attention of the Social Services Committee together with the need to reduce the case loads of Social Workers. Likewise the case loads of the Health Visitors should be greatly reduced.'

219. Prior to the Oakes Committee hearings Mrs Costello had discussions with some members of the Department's Management Team as to how Mr Pickstock should be presented to the Inquiry. It is not clear who actually took part in these discussions but we consider that it is likely that the Director was aware of them. We find that a deliberate decision was taken to minimise Mr Pickstock's weaknesses. This 'presentation' of Mr Pickstock was not only adopted before Oakes but also pervaded the early stages of Mrs Costello's evidence to us. The decision was no doubt motivated by a sense of loyalty to Mr Pickstock. There was a feeling, and a justified feeling, that Mr Pickstock was wrongly being set up as the scapegoat for the failings of others and the mischances of circumstances. It was also motivated by the defensive attitude of the Central Wirral Area Office and the Department as a whole when the subject of criticism. It had unfortunate results. The strain upon Mr Pickstock grew as did public unease.

220. Mr Pickstock's capabilities and weaknesses as a social worker were germane to any objective investigation of the Department's handling of the case of Paul and Liam from March to August 1976. His drinking habits, his laxity in recording, his distaste for routine work and the suggestion that he was given to making half-truths about visiting clients were all relevant to a balanced assessment as to whether or not they affected his judgement and thoroughness when overseeing Paul and Liam. It was for the Oakes Committee who were hearing the matter in private to decide for themselves the relevance of these matters and put them in perspective. Over two years later we had to hear evidence about these matters in public.

**The 'Missing Memo'**

221. Among the matters which led to the setting up of our Inquiry was the suggestion made in some quarters that Mr Pickstock had written a memorandum for his superiors in March 1976 in which he had asserted that Stanley and Sarah were unsuitable people to have the care of Paul and Liam. If Mr Pickstock had written any such memorandum it was not heeded by his superiors and they would therefore have been open to criticism. The suggestion went further. It was alleged that the memorandum had been in the possession of some member of the Social Services Department during the Oakes Inquiry but had been deliberately withheld from that Inquiry. After the Oakes Inquiry it was suggested that the alleged memorandum was deliberately suppressed; in effect, that there was a cover up.

222. These suggestions had grave consequences. The Social Services Department from top to bottom had to continue working in an atmosphere of suspicion and mistrust. Certain Councillors lost confidence in the Department and its management. Rumour and defamatory innuendo became rife. Tales of the 'missing memo' were reported in the media. **Although we have**

**come to the firm conclusion that neither Mr Pickstock nor anyone else made any such memorandum and that therefore it was not withheld from the Oakes Inquiry or later suppressed it is necessary for us to examine in some detail the evidence relating to the alleged memorandum to dispel for good the false rumours.** We feel that such rumours gained credence and widespread circulation because the Social Services Department had lost its integrity and thus the confidence of the Council.

223. The Oakes Inquiry held its first meeting on the 27th February 1978. The Inquiry lasted 4 days. On the 1st March 1978, the penultimate day of the Oakes Inquiry, the hearings took place in the Wallasey Town Hall in Committee Room 4. At about 8 pm on that day a caucus meeting of Conservative Councillors took place in the same room. An early arrival at the meeting was Councillor Ken Allen, then Vice-Chairman of the Social Services Committee. He noticed two piles of documents on separate tables in the room. We find that Councillor Ken Allen paid little attention to the piles of documents. Two later arrivals were Councillor Mrs Wood and Councillor Walker, both members of the Social Services Committee. They were sitting next to Councillor David Allan; on the table in front of him was one of the piles of documents. From idle curiosity he flicked through the documents and noticed a consultant's report, by Dr Vernon Jones. He pushed the papers aside where they were looked at with greater interest by Councillor Mrs Wood and Councillor Walker. Councillor Mrs Wood noticed the consultant's report. She knew Dr Vernon Jones. She also saw, as did Councillor Walker, a large brown envelope marked 'confidential' and addressed to Mr McDermott. The documents were Area Health Authority documents and they were photostat copies. Area Health Authority documents were not distributed to social workers at the Inquiry.

224. One document, which has come to be known as the 'missing memo', aroused Councillor Walker's attention. He described it as a clear typewritten document on one sheet of A4 size paper typed on both sides with the typing about three quarters of the way down on the reverse side of the page. It was clearly headed 'Paul and Liam Brown' which was underlined. It was clearly marked 'From A Pickstock' whom Councillor Walker knew to be the social worker in the Paul Brown case. It was dated the 23rd or the 27th March 1976. It ended with a recommendation, strongly worded, that because of the problems that the Brown family had had with their 9 children Paul and Liam should not be left with them. It was signed 'A Pickstock'. Councillor Walker gave Councillor Mrs Wood a dig in the ribs saying words to the effect of: 'Read that. It's dynamite'. He used this phrase because the document contained information which differed from his understanding of the case, derived no doubt in part from the Director's bland report of the 19th October 1977. Mrs Wood scanned the document and her recollection of its form was similar to that of Councillor Walker.

225. **We have considered the evidence of Councillor Walker and Councillor Mrs Wood and have reached the conclusion that they did not see any document of which we have not seen a copy.** We are satisfied that as witnesses they had no bias against the Social Services Department or any member of its staff. Not surprisingly after this length of time there were discrepancies in

their evidence as between each other and compared with what they said to the Heald Inquiry. We found them both honest and to the best of their ability careful and accurate. With the passing of time we think that Councillor Walker and to a very much lesser extent Councillor Mrs Wood have convinced themselves that the document that they saw was so lethal in content that it would have given a very different picture of the handling of the case in March and April 1976. **Our Conclusion is that the two Councillors misunderstood and misdescribed the document which they saw.**

226. We have not overlooked in reaching our conclusion that the two Councillors at the conclusion of the caucus meeting regarded the finding of the piles of papers, including a confidential consultant's report, as so important that the papers were taken to the Leader of the Council, Councillor Deverill, to whom Councillor Walker repeated in reference to the document which had aroused their attention that 'it was dynamite'. Nor have we overlooked the fact that when five weeks later Councillor Walker received his copy of the Oakes report he made comments in the margin referring to Mr Pickstock's report and the date March 1976, and at the Committee meeting considering the Oakes report on the 10th April 1978 both Councillors immediately referred to the absence in the report of any reference to the document that they had seen.

227. **The main reason why we do not accept the Councillors' description of the document is that we believed Mr Pickstock when he gave evidence to us stating that he neither signed nor made any such memorandum.** The existence of such a document is inconsistent with the contemporary carbon copy of the original running record in the day file which ended with the entry which reads:

> '26.3.76 visit, children satisfactory. No knowledge of where Mrs Brown is, decided to let Order lapse, advised Mrs Costello SSW accordingly'.

Its existence is inconsistent with all other documents that we have seen, including the addendum to the Social Enquiry Report on Stephen Brown which was prepared by Mr Pickstock on the 24th March 1976, and its contents are not even hinted at in any other document. It was not in keeping with Mr Pickstock's style of working to have prepared any such memorandum.

228. If Mr Pickstock had in March 1976 held the views attributed to him in the alleged 'memo' we would have expected him to have communicated his opinion to Mrs Doran when he spoke to her on the telephone on the 22nd June. If he had made a recommendation that Paul and Liam should not be allowed to continue staying with Stanley and Sarah and that recommendation had been rejected by Mrs Costello or some other Senior we would have expected him to have mentioned the facts to Councillor Mrs Wood when they met by chance in the 'Clarence' in August 1976. They were near neighbours and their daughters were school friends. If he had made such a recommendation we would have expected him to grasp this 'life-line' which would have prevented much of the criticism of him.

229. We cannot imagine in what circumstances such a supposedly lethal document could be brought to the Oakes Inquiry and be left loose with a

pile of photostat copy documents. If by chance someone had discovered such a document we cannot envisage the circumstances in which he would leave it lying about. We would have expected the finder to have pocketed it.

230. We are unable to make a precise finding as to which document the Councillors saw. No document comes within all of their descriptions even allowing for the the differences in those descriptions. There are however several documents which we saw, one of which may have been the document seen by the Councillors. The existence of the envelope addressed to Mr McDermott does not exist; the evidence was that Mr McDermott sent out from the Oakes Committee hearing a request for some staff structure plans which may have been delivered in that envelope.

231. The evidence was that all documents used at the Oakes Inquiry including those supplied by the Area Health Authority were photostats. Bearing in mind the provenance of the alleged 'missing memo' when discovered by the Councillors we would have expected it to have been a document in the possession of the Area Health Authority. A candidate for such a document is Mrs Doran's report for Dr Vernon Jones dated the 30th June 1976. This is likely to have been located in the pile of papers close to his report dated the 22nd June 1976 to Dr Vaughan Roberts. Mrs Doran's report does refer thrice on the last page to Mr Pickstock by name and states that Mr Pickstock:

> 'considers both these little boys may well be received into care once again. He was not entirely happy that their mother sought their discharge from care . . . . considers the conjugal relationship between the younger Mrs Brown and David Brown to be unstable . . . Mr Pickstock has been supervising the family now for some months. He considers that the grandmother copes reasonably and that she is well experienced in child management, having reared some 18 children of her own, but he feels that to accept these two when she is now well into her middle age may well prove too heavy a burden . . . '

The argument against this document being the 'missing memo' is that it is not signed 'A. Pickstock'.

232. Several documents signed 'A Pickstock' were produced to us. None of them fitted in content anything described by the Councillors although one, a Social History Report prepared for the case conference on the 17th August 1976, did have a last entry dated 'On 5 March 1976'. At the end of the caucus meeting the two piles of documents were handed to Councillor Deverill who put them on his desk in his room in the Wallasey Town Hall. He locked the door of the room. Next morning he telephoned Mr Samuels, the personal assistant to the Chief Executive, who had been responsible for arranging the setting up of the Oakes Inquiry. Mr Samuels visited the Inquiry each day before the hearing began and again at lunch-time to ask the Chairman if he required anything. Councillor Deverill asked Mr Samuels to collect the documents from his room, saying that the key to his room could be obtained from the hall porter. Councillor Deverill told Mr Samuels to return the papers to Mr Douglas Jones and at the same time to deliver to him a rebuke for leaving confidential papers about. Later on the evening of the same day Mr

Samuels told Councillor Deverill that he had done as he had been asked, but that the papers were Mr McDermott's and not Mr Douglas Jones'.

**The Price-Jones investigation**

233. When the Oakes report was discussed by the Social Services Committee on the 10th April 1978, the question of the 'missing memo' was raised. As a consequence and after consultation with the Chairman of the Social Services Committee the Chief Executive asked Mr Price-Jones, the Deputy Director of Administration and Legal Services, to carry out an inquiry as to the existence and whereabouts of the 'missing-memo'. Mr Douglas Jones was not given prior notice of the Price-Jones investigation and it only became general knowledge within the Department after Mr Price-Jones had interviewed the first witness, Mrs Costello. Mr Douglas Jones and his whole Department were naturally upset at what they considered to be an assumption by the Council that they had been guilty of foul play. Mr Douglas Jones wanted the police brought in and with the atmosphere prevailing in the Social Services Department at this time we can understand this desire. We do not however think that the introduction of the police would have helped in solving the mystery. Mr Douglas Jones' request to bring in the police was refused and the Price-Jones inquiry continued with almost all the witnesses insisting on having their solicitor present when interviewed. The conclusion of the Price-Jones inquiry was that the existence of the 'missing memo' could not be proved. **In our opinion the conclusion of the Price-Jones inquiry was reasonable, on the evidence available, but we feel that the way in which the investigation was set up and handled was clumsy.**

234. The scope of the Price-Jones inquiry extended beyond its original ambit because Mr Douglas Jones and Mr McDermott both said that they had never been handed the pile of documents which had been left in Councillor Deverill's locked room. They said the same to us and we believe them. The result was that, allegedly, not only a 'missing memo' but also a whole pile of documents had been spirited away; this deepened the atmosphere of mutual mistrust. The responsibility for this we find lies with Mr Samuels. We find that when he said on the late evening of the 2nd March 1978 to Councillor Deverill that he had done as he had been asked he told a fib. When faced with the denials of Mr Douglas Jones and Mr McDermott he gave a different and false account of his handling of the documents. We feel it our duty, in fairness to the Social Services Department, to go into this matter in some detail because the suspicion rested on the Department that they disposed of the documents for sinister reasons. Committee Room 4 the Leader's room and Mr Samuels' room were within about thirty yards of each other in Wallasey Town Hall. On the morning that Mr Samuels received Councillor Deverill's instruction, around 10.00 am, the Oakes Inquiry was due to sit in about a quarter of an hour. If Mr Samuels had intended to carry out Councillor Deverill's express instructions we would have expected him to have unlocked Councillor Deverill's room, taken the papers to Committee Room 4 when the Inquiry started, and handed them to Mr Douglas Jones along with the rebuke, or to Mr McDermott if Mr Douglas Jones was absent, in case the papers were required that day. Indeed on that very morning Mr McDermott gave evidence to the Oakes Committee followed by Mr Douglas

Jones who was part-heard at lunchtime. Later in the afternoon Mr Holt, the Chief Executive, gave evidence. The Inquiry ended at about 3.30 pm.

235. On the 25th April 1978 Mr Samuels made a signed statement saying:

> 'I collected the key of the Leader's room from Mr Swinburn and found a folder, which I think was red in colour, which was full of papers and which I assumed to be photocopies of documents distributed at the inquiry. I did not open the folder or read any of the papers. Later that day, or possibly the following day, I told Mr Jones about the papers and gave him Councillor Deverill's "message". Mr Jones told me that the papers belonged to Mr McDermott and I later returned the folder—I believe to Mr Jones, although it may have possibly been to Mr McDermott. I am afraid I cannot recall'.

This account was denied by Mr Douglas Jones and Mr McDermott. On the 24th May 1978 Councillor Wells told Mr Samuels that no member of the Council would accept his version of events. On the 25th May 1978 Mr Samuels telephoned Mrs Burford, who was Mr Douglas Jones' secretary, at a time when Mr Douglas Jones was out at an Area Health Authority meeting. Mrs Burford made a contemporary note of her telephone conversation. After she had told Mr Samuels that she expected Mr Douglas Jones to be out for the afternoon Mr Samuels asked her if she would mind him asking her a question. She replied 'No'. He then asked her when she started work for the Director. She replied March. He then asked her who was in the office in February. She told him that there was a temporary lady and someone who had left since she was appointed. We think that the purpose of Mr Samuels in asking these questions was to spy out the land.

236. Mr Samuels' second written statement is dated the 5th June 1978 in which he says:

> '. . . I am now writing to confirm that I have remembered what I did with the file. I took it over to give to Mr Jones at his office on Thursday, 2nd March. I have reached this date by process of elimination because I am sure it was not on the Friday when the enquiry proper had concluded and it could not have been any earlier. My impression is that I took the file across at lunchtime. I went into the office of Mr Jones's secretary and there were two ladies in the room one seated at the desk and the other, I think, standing with her back to the window. I asked for Mr Jones and was told that he was still out. I therefore asked the lady sitting at the desk, who as far as I remember was a youngish lady, if she would hand the file to Mr Jones on his return and tell him that this was the file of which he and I had been speaking earlier . . .'

237. Mr Samuels gave evidence to us on the lines of this statement. We found his evidence wholly unconvincing and reject it. He was unable to give any rational explanation for going to Birkenhead with the file instead of handing it in to Committee Room 4. We heard evidence from all the typists who could have been in Mr Douglas Jones' secretary's office at the time when Mr Samuels claims to have taken the file over to Birkenhead. None of these typists had any recollection of Mr Samuels' visit.

238. Mr McDermott gave evidence to us that on one day during the Oakes Inquiry a man, he thought a porter, put his hand round the door with a bundle of papers saying that they belonged to the Committee. Mr McDermott handed these papers to the Committee Clerk. **We accept Mr McDermott's evidence and find that that bundle of papers was the same as that entrusted by Councillor Deverill to Mr Samuels. Thereafter that bundle of papers, probably all photostats, got lost in the welter of papers before the Committee.**

239. We have considered a number of possible explanations for Mr Samuels' fib and all the embarrassing consequences. The probable explanation is that he could not face passing on a rebuke to a Chief Officer of the Council, Mr Douglas Jones being very much his superior in the hierarchy. He therefore delegated the task of delivering the papers to a porter.

**The Heald Inquiry**

240. Following the Price-Jones inquiry the Wirral Borough Council decided to establish an independent inquiry:

> 'into a claim that the material document which was not put in evidence before the panel of inquiry investigating the conduct of the Paul and Liam Brown case existed at the time of the inquiry'.

This second independent inquiry was held on the 25th July 1978 before Mr Mervyn Heald, QC. The Heald Inquiry was not a statutory inquiry and therefore Mr Heald had no power to enforce the presence of witnesses. In advance of the hearing 36 employees of the Council and several Councillors were invited to attend the hearing for the purpose of giving evidence. The staff of the Council however decided, on the advice of NALGO, not to give evidence. This lack of co-operation proved a severe handicap to Mr Heald but he nevertheless decided to continue. In his report dated the 6th October 1978 he concluded that a typewritten report by Mr Pickstock stating that Stanley and Sarah were not suitable persons to continue to have the custody of Paul and Liam was in existence in March 1976, and that this report was not shown to the Oakes Inquiry. Mr Heald also noted that the running record had been 'skilfully changed' to purport to show that the decision to leave the children where they were was a joint one of Mr Pickstock and Mrs Costello. Mr Heald raised the question of whether, and to what extent, the Oakes Inquiry had been misled and he suggested that the Council might:

> 'wish to consider whether to make a formal request to the Secretary of State for an enquiry to be held under Section 98 (1)(a) of the Children Act, 1975'.

## CHAPTER TEN

# THE HANDLING OF THE PAUL BROWN CASE

### The need for an investigation

241. By the time of the case conference of the 17th August 1976 the Social Services Department had learnt that Paul Brown was critically ill and that in the opinion of Mr Miles, the consultant neurosurgeon in charge of Paul at Walton Hospital, it was a case of non-accidental injury. The staff of the Department were aware that they had known Paul and his family since the Department's inception. They knew that failures in communication and case appreciation had occurred. Mrs Sayer, the health visitor, had been unable to trace Paul and Liam's whereabouts. The social worker's case file had been mislaid on transmission from the Birkenhead Area Office. The Central Wirral Office had been unaware that the boys had been on the At Risk Register.

242. These circumstances demanded an immediate and searching investigation with the object of discovering what mistakes were made, what were the explanations for such mistakes and what improvements could be made in child care cases to reduce the risk of future similar tragedies. This investigation required a detailed analysis of all material facts. This analysis had to be critical and constructive and made without fear or favour to achieve credibility and thus acceptance.

243. Mrs Penk became entrusted with this task. It was suggested that she took the task of her own volition because she was the Specialist Child Care Officer. We find that the Department Management Team specifically gave her the responsibility not only because of her specialist knowledge of child care procedures but also because she had ready access to the Director whose office was opposite hers in the headquarters building.

244. Mrs Penk, in the reports that she prepared for internal consumption by the Department Management Team and the Director, displayed a large measure of objectivity and thoroughness. These reports show her considerable knowledge of child care procedures and have a proper balance of criticism, explanation and constructive suggestion. Thoroughness and balance are however strikingly lacking in two very important reports. In March 1977 a report, in the form of an historical narrative of the Department's involvement, was prepared for the Chairman of the Social Services Committee. A copy was handed to the DHSS. This report omitted mention of certain important facts which could have laid the Department open to valid criticism. In October 1977 Mrs Penk drafted another report which contained the conclusion that no member of the Department's staff could be validly criticised in all the circumstances; this report also contained significant omissions of fact. We find that the October 1977 report with its bland conclusion, which any objective analysis of the facts demonstrates is ill-founded, was deliberately drafted to allay criticism. We find that contrary to what Mrs Penk told us, no doubt through a sense of loyalty to her superiors, both these reports were drafted from guidelines laid down by the Department Management Team who set their tone and bias and were responsible for the major omissions of fact.

The second report was delivered by Mr Douglas Jones to the Social Services Committee of the 19th October 1977. It was a deliberate attempt to mislead the Committee. The results were disastrous for the Department and its staff. The Department Management Team lost credibility. The Oakes Inquiry was set up and the criticisms of the Social Services Department made in the Oakes report were heavily publicised in the press.

245. Management should not have deputed to Mrs Penk the responsibility of investigation. She was personally disqualified since she herself was personally involved in the case through her failure to ensure a review of Paul and Liam on the At Risk Register in April 1976. When Paul was admitted to hospital she must have realised that she was open to criticism. That is why, in our opinion, she hurried over to Central Wirral at 9 am on the 13th August 1976 to find out what they knew. In our opinion it is significant that it was not until our Inquiry that Mrs Penk's personal involvement was revealed. She frankly admitted that she had never told anyone of this personal involvement before nor mentioned it in any of her reports. This omission is a typical symptom of lack of professional confidence and security.

246. Mrs Penk was also disqualified by reason of her grade which was similar to that of a Deputy Area Officer. In the case of Paul and Liam many social workers of similar and superior grade to Mrs Penk had taken decisions or been involved in incidents which required evaluation. Mr Douglas Jones himself and Mr McDermott had become involved at the time when the boys were placed on the At Risk Register in March/April 1975. Mr Hotchkiss was directly involved in the problem of Pauline's demands for the return of Paul and Liam and so were Mr Wylde and Mrs Gurny. Thus Mrs Penk was placed in an invidious position.

**Public inquiries**

247. The failure to establish an immediate independent investigation aimed at finding the truth and making constructive criticism caused the mistrust and misunderstandings of the ensuing years. It has culminated in our Inquiry at vast public expense and private anguish for the many witnesses who appeared before us and for their families. Money, time and effort which should have been spent in providing better social services in the Wirral have been wasted in the years since 1976 on sterile recriminations, discussions and inquiries. Much time has been devoted to trivial disputes which over the years have developed into matters of principle in the eyes of the participants. In recent years there have been a large number of inquiries following the death of a child known to a Social Services Department; indeed our Inquiry is the second such public statutory inquiry to be held on Merseyside in the last two years. The necessity for such inquiries of the quasi-judicial kind only arises when public disquiet justifiably demands one. This should be only in the most exceptional circumstances. **It is our strong opinion that formal inquiries, whether public like ours or private like the Oakes Inquiry, should not come to be regarded as the normal method of investigating the circumstances which have led to serious injury to a child known to a Social Services Department.** However vociferous the demands for such an inquiry may be from the local public or media not only are such inquiries time-consuming and expensive

but the threat of them may inhibit social workers in the field. Their daily work requires personal and independent decisions and even the taking of risks after making considered judgements based on experience and professional training. Occasionally the future may prove that a social worker's decision was wrong. With hindsight it may have been but if viewed objectively at the time it was made it might have been judged as courageous and constructive. Tragedies have occurred and will continue not to be prevented, through bad luck, human fallibility or minor lapses in procedures often by very junior and inexperienced staff. If every time this occurs a Social Services Department or other related agency is put through a wide ranging quasi-judicial inquiry, exposing individual social workers to the anxiety of inquiries inevitably prolonged and delayed and at times to unjustified public obloquy, the confidence of the social work profession will be undermined and the quality of its services to the community reduced. **It should also be remembered that the responsibility for the death of a non-accidentally injured child lies with the person who caused the injuries; we cannot and should not 'blame' the social worker for having failed to prevent a tragedy from occurring.**

248. If a tragedy does occur, the public rightly require an investigation. **The investigation must command the confidence of the public. If an investigation appears to be inspired by a desire to exonerate the Social Services Department or individual members of its staff rather than the intention to achieve an objective and detailed analysis of the facts coupled with constructive criticism the public will rightly not be satisfied.**

**The conduct of investigations**

249. In our opinion, Directors of Social Services Departments and heads of other related agencies who have the responsibility of dealing with the death or injury of a child should have in mind the following considerations. We stress that these are not rules or guidelines, they are matters to be thought about. No two cases will ever be the same. There will be some cases which at the outset clearly call for disciplinary procedures in which instances the following considerations would be inappropriate:

a. As soon as a tragedy becomes known the Director must call in and secure all relevant files and documents, to prevent the alteration of records and to protect the staff from wrongful accusations of falsification or alteration of documents.

b. the investigator must have the right approach. His approach should be: what were the facts and what lessons for the future can be learnt? His approach should never be: who was to blame and what excuses can be put forward? If the former approach is adopted and known to the investigated the people concerned are likely to be frank and the investigation profitable, otherwise the investigator is likely to meet with half truths, concealments or silences and his investigation becomes inconclusive.

c. The appropriate authority must appoint the right person as investigator. In Social Services Departments he should be of second or third tier status. The investigator should never be inquiring into his seniors or equals. This does not mean that the cannot have assistants, particularly in specialist procedures, but the responsibility for and conduct of the investigation must remain directly his. Occasionally it would be inappropriate for the investigator to the appointed from within a Social Services Department because of the personal involvement of senior management in the handling of a particular case. This is an example of such a case. Both Mr Douglas Jones and Mr McDermott had been personally involved. In such instances the Director could invite the Director of Social Services of some nearby authority to nominate an appropriate investigator or approach the Association of Directors of Social Services for their nomination. Sometimes the investigations cannot be confined to scrutiny of the activities of the Social Services Department. It may involve, as in this case, health visitors and doctors. In such cases the investigation will have to be multi-disciplinary to be worthwhile. In some instances the Director may consider it appropriate to ask the Area Review Committee to nominate a co-ordinating investigator who must be acceptable to the various disciplines involved. We note that para. 12g. of DHSS Circular LASSL (74)13 'Non-Accidental Injury to Children', in dealing with the role of Area Review Committees, states that the ARC should 'advise on the need for inquiries into cases which appear to have gone wrong and from which lessons could be learned'.

d. The investigator must be wholly independent. He must not have had any personal involvement with the case, as unfortunately was the case with Mrs Penk.

e. The investigator should carry out his task informally. he should see all witnesses singly, in private and in confidence. It should be made known that no question of apportioning blame or of taking disciplinary procedures shall arise. This undertaking should be given before any witness is seen. In these circumstances anything said by the witness to the investigator would be inadmissible in any other proceedings. In taking statements and making notes of interviews he himself should take them down in longhand. The notes should not be copied or typed or circulated. They should be kept securely in the personal custody of the investigator and they should be destroyed by the investigator as soon as his report has been considered by the Social Services Committee and relevant agencies. If witnesses are assured that their evidence is confidential to the investigator, and will not be revealed by him, they are more likely to be frank. **The relevant agencies should be aware of the implications of this policy and willing to support this constructive approach rather than to seek scapegoats.**

f. If the investigator considers it fit to make any criticism of anyone in his report he should, before his report is submitted, show the relevant passage in his report to the person concerned, discuss it with him and amend his report as appropriate or note any explanation or reservation by the person concerned.

g. The report should as far as possible refer to people by their jobs or positions and not by names.

h. The investigator should work fast and full-time on the investigation. Delay increases the risk of faulty recollection and the spread of rumour.

i. The report should remain confidential to the appropriate agencies who should consider it in private, although in some special cases it may be appropriate to publish the broad conclusions of a report.

## CHAPTER ELEVEN

# THE DIRECTOR OF SOCIAL SERVICES AND WIRRAL BOROUGH COUNCIL

250. When **Mr Douglas Jones** arrived in the Wirral in November 1973 he was the outsider. Alone among all the Directors of Departments he had not been a member of one of the constituent authorities which became Wirral. He was the only Director who was not 'running down' one Department while building up a new one and his experience of local government was very limited. In his youth he had been a professional boxer. In those days he developed an interest in welfare work. His work was mainly in voluntary organisations, for example doing enterprising work for large university settlements. He spent a year in the Cabinet Office. By his own efforts he has achieved considerable academic honours over the years. In 1969 he entered local government at the top, as the Director of Social Services in Falkirk. He later moved to Stoke on Trent, and on local government reorganisation, to Wirral. He had therefore had no experience in the lower echelons of local government. His rivals, as they sadly became, had spent a working lifetime in local government but their backgrounds were more orthodox and limited. Mr Douglas Jones gave evidence to us over seven days and many documents of which he was the author were produced. Many of the witnesses spoke of their relationships with him. We thus had ample material upon which to assess him both as a man and as a Director of Social Services.

251. Mr Douglas Jones is intelligent, pugnacious, determined and imaginative. He has a genuine concern for those in need. His vision of social work is expansionist and experimental. The general attitude of his subordinates shows that he is able to inspire loyalty. This is in itself recognition by them of his professionalism and genuine care for the value of their work. We experienced the present efficiency and humanity of his Department not only throughout the 10 weeks of evidence and submissions but also on our visits to the Department's headquarters and Area Offices. Against these qualities must be set Mr Douglas Jones' weaknesses. He is quick to take offence and to see a slight where none may be intended. He reacts to criticism by counter-attack. He takes personally any criticism of his policy or his Department. Like other over-sensitive people he is less than sensitive when dealing with others.

252. Two examples illustrate his tendency to see offence when none was intended. In June 1977 Mr Betteridge, a Principal Solicitor in the Department of Administration and Legal Services, was contacted by a Social Services Department Area Officer about two children who were in care but had been removed illegally and taken to London. Mr Betteridge spent many hours working on the case, including attempting to obtain a writ of Habeas Corpus. During this time, over a weekend, he telephoned London many times, and also spoke to the Area Officer, the Deputy Director of Social Services, the Chairman of the Social Services Committee and many others. On the Monday morning Mr Douglas Jones' reaction was to send the Director of Administration and Legal Services rather a curt note:

'I understand that on Friday last you contacted the Chairman regarding a difficulty that had cropped up when an officer from this Department visited [a battered wives hostel], and I shall be glad if you will let me know why you took this action rather than approach myself or my Deputy.

This particular matter was nothing really out of the ordinary and I am at a loss to know why you took this action'.

253. The second example of over-reaction occurred when the Oakes report was sent to the Council and the Area Health Authority. A special meeting of the Area Review Committee was called for the 19th April 1978 to consider the report. The Council was also meeting that day and it was proposed that the Council should refer the report to the ARC for comment. It was therefore agreed between the Area Administrator of the Wirral Area Health Authority and the Council's Chief Executive that the ARC meeting should be postponed. Mr Samuels informed the Director of this decision during a lunch at the Area Health Authority and Mr Douglas Jones took great exception to the decision having been taken without consultation with him.

254. The problems of relationships within the Borough Council are well illustrated by five interlinked issues: the 'key areas' exercise; a DHSS study of the Social Services Department; the O and M studies of the Department; the post of Assistant Director (Forward Planning); and the proposal to close the Deeside Area Office.

**The 'Key Areas' Study**

255. At an early stage in the life of the new Wirral Borough Council Chief Officers were asked to produce 'position statements', setting out the activities of each Department and detailing the state of progress towards Departmental aims. On the basis of these statements Directors were then asked to prepare priority lists, ranking service areas according to their comparative level of need for more resources. In February 1976, while discussing the 1976/77 budget, the Policy and Resources Committee decided to ask each Chief Officer to prepare a list of areas worthy of in-depth study. The intention was to discover areas where economies could be made (category 1) in order to finance the current level of provision (category 2) or even an improvement (category 3) in other areas. Not all the resources saved by the economies in category 1 would be used on the other two categories—there would be an overall saving—but the intention was to devise a more rational approach to savings than the usual method of a universal percentage cut.

256. In the Spring and Summer of 1976 the Chief Executive (Mr Holt) and Director of Finance (Mr Rothwell) discussed with programme Directors the selection of areas worthy of study and the allocation of subjects to the three categories. In June 1976 the Director of Social Services produced his list of 'key areas' which included administration in the Social Services Department in category 2. Directors had been asked to specify what kind of study was required for each key area and Mr Douglas Jones had proposed an O and M study for social services administration. The Chief Executive, in discussion with the Director of Finance, the Leader of the Council, and the Chair-

man of the Social Services Committee, felt that an external study would be preferable because:

a. O and Ms were not popular in the Social Services Department; and

b. if the study resulted in a recommendation for increased resources such advice would be better given from 'outside'.

Management consultants were costly and in any case did not have any specialist knowledge of social services and the Director of Finance therefore suggested the use of the DHSS. The Chief Executive approached the DHSS and was referred to the Department's Regional Social Work Service in Manchester. Having made the initial approaches Mr Holt wrote to Mr Hannan, the Principal Social Work Service Officer North West Region, and informed the Director of Social Services that he had done so. Mr Douglas Jones was thus informed of the decision to call in the DHSS to examine his Department after the request to the DHSS had been made. We believe this was a mistake on Mr Holt's part and that Mr Douglas Jones should have been a party to the discussions on this important matter.

**The DHSS Study**

257. The first meeting between Mr Hannan and the authority was held in July 1976 and it appears to have been somewhat heated. Mr Hannan gained the impression that the study was to be part of a savings exercise but this may have been the result of a confusion over the three categories since he was also told that if more resources were called for the Council would be willing to provide them. Following further meetings in July and August 1976 Mr Hannan attended a meeting in September at which the proposed study was greeted favourably by the unions. At this time NALGO were given an undertaking that they could see Mr Hannan's report and submit their comments alongside those of the Council's officers to the Social Services Committee in due course. This undertaking later became the source of some friction between Mr Douglas Jones and Mr Holt.

258. In November 1976 the DHSS team undertook their study. On the 20th November the West Cheshire News carried an item in which Mr Holt was quoted as saying that the DHSS had been brought in because:

> 'we are not sure whether we have got the organisation right within the social services department, particularly at the senior administrative levels'.

Mr Holt did not consult with Mr Douglas Jones before making this comment to the press and we feel that such a comment was unlikely to improve morale in the Social Services Department.

259. The study having been completed Mr Hannan discussed the results with the Director of Social Services and with the Chairman of the Social Services Committee and various Chief Officers. On the 7th January 1977 Mr Hannan sent his report, comprising 4 pages, to the Chief Executive. The authority had hoped for something more detailed and Mr Hannan was persuaded to supply Mr Holt with the study team's background notes, for very limited circulation. The Social Services Committee meeting of the 9th February 1977 was provided with the short report only and the Chairman was requested to obtain Mr Hannan's permission for the Committee to see the additional

notes. Mr Hannan agreed to this and attended a meeting of the Committee on the 22nd February to explain his team's findings. NALGO had meanwhile been supplied with the short report and their comments were submitted to the 22nd February meeting (before Mr Douglas Jones had had an opportunity to see them).

260. Mr Douglas Jones told us that from the time when he had first heard of the decision to call in the DHSS he had regarded the study as an attempt to discredit the Social Services Department and himself in particular. Mr Holt assured us that this was never the intention and that the decision to set up the study was the result of a general concern over deficiencies in administration in the Department. He told us that Mr Douglas Jones had himself expressed concern about the abilities of the Assistant Director (Administration) and recognised the need to improve the performance of the administrative staff. According to Mr Holt the Social Services Committee had also expressed criticisms of this aspect of the Department's organisation. Although administration in the Department was a category 2 study, implying that the maintenance of the existing level of service was a priority, Mr Douglas Jones told us that the Chief Executive and Director of Finance gave him the impression that they were looking for savings. Whatever the origins of the study the final result was clearly something of a disappointment. Mr Hannan had warned Mr Holt that the DHSS Social Work Service had no expertise in administrative procedures and the Director of Personnel and Management Services told us that he had been unhappy at the use of the DHSS to conduct the study in the first place. Certainly the entire episode made a significant contribution to the widening gulf between Mr Douglas Jones on the one hand and Mr Holt and Mr Roberts (the Chairman of the Social Services Committee) on the other.

**O and M Studies**

261. One of the results of the DHSS study was that on the 17th March 1977 the Social Services Committee recommended an organisation and methods (O and M) study of administrative procedures and the allocation of administrative responsibilities within the Social Services Department; this was the continuation of an unhappy saga.

262. Within the first four months of the new authority in 1974 the Director of Personnel and Management Services (DPMS) was asked to commission an immediate O and M review into the necessity of (a) unfreezing three Specialist Officer posts and (b) creating a new post of Principal Assistant to the Assistant Director (Fieldwork) in the Social Services Department. This was to be followed by an O and M review of staffing requirements generally within the Fieldwork division, bearing in mind the need to second social work staff for training. In December 1974 the Policy and Resources Committee approved the new Principal Assistant post (among a number of others) and proposed an O and M review of all the Council's Departments, starting with Housing and Environmental Health, and Social Services. In February 1975 two of the three Specialist Officer posts were unfrozen and in April 1975 approval was given for various regradings and for up to 15 staff to be seconded per year. Despite these improvements there was a general opposition to O and

M studies from the staff of the Social Services Department and in April 1975 NALGO banned all further O and Ms until November 1975. As soon as the ban was lifted the DPMS arranged an O and M of transport utilisation, at the request of Mr Douglas Jones. In November 1976 NALGO imposed a further ban until March 1977. It was against this background that the Social Services Committee received the report of the DHSS study.

263. Following the Social Services Committee's recommendation on the 17th March 1977 it was agreed that O and M should review the whole of the Social Services Department starting in headquarters with (a) personnel and training and (b) salaries and wages. These two studies began on the 18th May 1977 and were completed in August and October 1977 respectively. Mr Douglas Jones agreed the recommendations of the personnel and training review in principle but disagreed with the proposal to locate the new staffing section, headed by a Senior Administrative Officer, within the command of the Assistant Director (Administration). Mr Douglas Jones wanted the new section placed under the new Principal Assistant (Personnel and Training). Because of this disagreement the salaries and wages review was not accepted until February 1978 and the personnel and training review was not finalised until April 1978. Meanwhile an O and M of the finance function of the Social Services Department was begun in November 1977 and completed in February 1978. This review recommended the appointment of a new Assistant Director (Forward Planning) and the DPMS felt that a post of Assistant Director (Special Services) was also required.

**The Assistant Director (Forward Planning)**

264. Since 1976 the workload of the Social Services Department and in particular of the Director had increased dramatically. The Chairman of the Social Services Committee, Councillor Roberts, was demanding a considerable amount of the Director's attention. At the same time the Director was involved in the key area studies, the DHSS study, and in developing the strategy for health care. In view of this increased workload and in order to delegate much of the routine work Mr Douglas Jones had asked for a personal assistant. This request was rejected.

265. Following the DHSS study the Council felt that the Director was overloaded with work. Three major areas were identified which were directly accountable to and required the detailed involvement of the Director (Community Services and Development, Forward Planning and Research, and Area Health Liaison). This was felt by both the Council and the Director to be unsatisfactory and discussions about the problem took place between Mr Douglas Jones, the Director of Finance and the Director of Personnel and Management Services. Mr Rothwell (the Director of Finance), suggested the appointment of an Assistant Director (Forward Planning and Development) to relieve Mr Douglas Jones of much of the pressure of work in the problem areas and to allow him more time for his primary task of overall responsibility for the Department. Mr Douglas Jones did not agree with Mr Rothwell; he felt that the suggestion was an attempt to remove one of the existing Assistant Directors and as such he opposed it.

266. On the 21st June 1978 the Council confirmed the establishment of two additional Assistant Director posts (Assistant Director (Forward Planning and Development) and Assistant Director (Special Services)). The three existing Assistant Directors were opposed to the creation of the new posts; they felt that the introduction of two additional Assistant Directors would weaken their case for the regrading of their posts. (The three existing Assistant Directors were awaiting the end of the Government pay policy before their posts could be upgraded).

267. In an attempt to compromise, Mr Douglas Jones suggested an alternative proposal which involved the regrading of the three existing Assistant Director posts and the introduction of three additional posts:

Principal Co-Ordinator (Forward Planning and Development);

Principal Assistant (Special Services); and

Principal Assistant (Residential and Day Care).

The recommendation for a Principal Co-Ordinator (Forward Planning and Development) who would work directly to the Director was supported by the Director of Personnel but on the 25th September 1978 the recommendation was rejected by the Social Services Committee who insisted that the appointment be made at Assistant Director level, as originally proposed by Mr Rothwell.

268. The appointment of an Assistant Director (Forward Planning and Development) was approved by the Council in April 1979, subject to consultations with NALGO. These consultations and discussions were still taking place and the post had still not been filled at the time of our Inquiry. Clearly the negotiations have been difficult but this delay in the implementation of Council policy can only have had an adverse effect on the relationship between the Director of Social Services and the Council.

269. The final O and M review resulting from the DHSS study was into the general administrative services of the Social Services Department. This review began in June 1978—Mr Douglas Jones having requested it be deferred in February 1978 because of problems in the Department connected with the Oakes Inquiry—and was completed in November 1978. At the time of our Inquiry this final review had not been discussed by Mr Douglas Jones with the Department of Personnel and Management Services. Mr Douglas-Jones has maintained throughout that O and M reviews should be just one of the tools available to management, and should not be imposed on a programme Director against his advice. He denied that he had been obstructive towards the O and M teams and said that once a report had been agreed by the Council he accepted it as Council policy and carried it out. It nonetheless appeared to us that when an O and M report was not to his liking Mr Douglas Jones resorted to delaying tactics which were often successful. We note, for example, that with the appointment of Mr SeQueira as Deputy Director the pressure to appoint the additional Assistant Directors, whom Mr Douglas Jones did not want, has abated. While criticising Mr Douglas Jones for delaying the implementation of O and M reports we note that the Department of Personnel and Management Services operated purely as an advisory service with no responsibility for ensuring that the O and M review team's

recommendations were workable in practice. **We suggest that programme Directors might be more willing to accept O and M reviews if the O and M teams were obliged to follow through their own recommendations and assist with their implementation.**

**The Deeside closure**

270. The proposal to close the Deeside Area Office caused a great deal of controversy and ill feeling within the Council. The proposal was first mooted in 1977 and was not finally abandoned until February 1980. In that time the proposed closure became a source of contention between Mr Douglas Jones and the rest of the Council.

271. The origin of the proposal to close Deeside is a matter of dispute. In preparation for the 1977/8 budget estimates Chief Officers were asked to prepare lists of options for savings of 20–25 per cent. This was a paper exercise—it was not intended to implement all the savings—and the Director of Social Services included the closure of 'an Area Office' in his list of options. Mr Douglas Jones claims that this option was seized on by the authority's management team (ie the Chief Officers) as a means of transferring staff from Deeside to the highly pressurized Birkenhead office. Under pressure from his colleagues he agreed that the proposal could be submitted to the caucus of the majority party. This pressure was denied by the other Chief Officers who gave evidence to us.

272. On the 1st March 1977 the Social Services Committee met to discuss their budget estimates for 1977/8 and when the meeting had finished the Chairman (Councillor Roberts) 'informally' announced the proposal to close the Deeside Office. Councillor Roberts had not consulted Mr Douglas Jones or warned him of his intention to announce the closure. Following this meeting the Director consulted the Deeside Area Officer and on the 21st March 1977 submitted a short report to the Committee suggesting that a full report be prepared if the Committee wished to go ahead with the closure. The Committee approved the closure in principle and asked the Director to work up full proposals. The Director of Administration and Legal Services (Mr Mills) then reminded Mr Douglas Jones that other Chief Officers had an interest in the future of Hoylake Town Hall, which housed the Deeside Office, and asked to be kept in touch. Some months later Mr Mills, having heard no more from Mr Douglas Jones, prepared his own report for the Social Services Committee meeting on the 25th May 1977. Mr Douglas Jones also submitted a report, on the possible redeployment of staff. The Committee reaffirmed its recommendation in principle subject to further consideration of the redeployment of staff and to the retention of an office facility in Deeside.

273. The closure proposal was then referred via the Policy and Resources Committee to the full Council. We deal with this stage in the history of the proposal in some detail because it provides an example of the difficulties which beset working relationships within the Wirral at that time.

274. Shortly before the Council meeting Councillor Roberts dropped in on a meeting between NALGO and the Director of Personnel. The NALGO

representatives took the opportunity of asking Councillor Roberts to 'take back' the Social Services Committee minute on Deeside when the minutes were discussed at Council. This would involve Councillor Roberts asking the Council for permission to refer the issue back to the Social Services Committee for further consideration. Councillor Roberts agreed to consider the request, he departed and returned 20 minutes later to say that he would take the minute back. On the evening of the Council meeting Mr Douglas Jones saw Councillor Roberts who appeared agitated. Having elicited the story of NALGO's involvement Mr Douglas Jones expressed his sorrow that the matter had been decided without reference to him. He advised Councillor Roberts that further uncertainty would be more damaging to staff morale than a firm and final decision to close Deeside. Councillor Roberts, according to Mr Douglas Jones, appeared to agree and made an unsuccessful attempt to contact NALGO. When the Social Services Committee minutes came up for discussion at Council Councillor Roberts made no move. During the next agenda item however the Chief Executive spoke to Councillor Roberts who then sought permission to return to the previous item and take the Deeside minute back. This was agreed by Council. The Deeside closure was thus once more open to discussion.

275. In the ensuing months the Social Services Committee reconsidered the matter and confirmed its decision of May 1977. The Director therefore worked on proposals for redrawing the boundaries of the 4 Area Offices which would remain. In January 1978 NALGO informed the Leader of the Council that if the Council approved the closure in principle the union would regard itself as in official dispute with the authority. After various meetings agreement was reached that NALGO would discuss boundaries for 4 Area Offices with the Director and on the 27th February 1978 the Leader of the Council wrote to NALGO confirming the agreement. The first meeting between NALGO and the Department was not held until the 21st September 1978 and the NALGO representatives at the meeting refused to discuss any proposals based on 4 Area Offices. NALGO put forward alternative proposals based on 5 Area Offices and Mr Douglas Jones agreed to discuss these. Mr Mills then wrote to Mr Douglas Jones expressing surprise that the agreement of the 27th February had been overturned and reminding him of the Leader's concern that the Council's instructions should not be contravened. On the 18th October 1978 the Social Services Committee instructed the Director to continue discussions on the boundaries for 4 Area Offices. The Staff Committee then broke off discussions with the Department and NALGO did not agree to resume discussions until February 1979.

276. In July 1979 the Director submitted a report to the Social Services Committee proposing 4 Area Offices plus two sub-offices at Heswall and Hoylake. Far from producing a saving this proposal would have resulted in increased expenditure. The Committee reaffirmed the proposal to close Deeside and instructed the Director to report back with proposals which would produce savings. It was not until September 1979 that the accommodation arrangements for the redeployed staff were considered or that an accurate costing of the closure proposal was produced. It then emerged that the proposals under discussion were unworkable. It was now clear that the only way to show a saving on the Deeside closure was to close Hoylake Town

Hall and this could not be done because other staff were housed in the building. In October 1979 Mr Douglas Jones sought advice on the dilemma—the Council had now set a deadline of December 1979 for the closure—from the Chief Executive. Mr Holt discussed the problem with the Leader and the Chairman of the Social Services Committee (now Councillor Leigh) and the latter suggested an alternative plan. On the 17th October 1979 the Director submitted a report to the Social Services Committee based on Councillor Leigh's new proposals and the Committee approved the new boundaries. The proposal to close Deeside was finally abandoned in February 1980.

277. The unhappy saga of the Deeside Office had a serious adverse effect on Mr Douglas Jones' relations with his political masters. The closure of Deeside was originally proposed as a savings exercise yet when the project was eventually costed it could not be made to show a saving. The members of the Council must inevitably have regarded the seemingly endless difficulties with NALGO as the result of delaying tactics on the part of Mr Douglas Jones. The final decision to keep Deeside open left the members of the Council with, as one witness put it, 'egg on their faces', an outcome which cannot have improved their opinion of Mr Douglas Jones.

278. The role of **the Chief Executive** is of the utmost importance in local government. He must give coherence to Council policy. He must harmonise the activities of the programme and servicing Departments. The programme Departments are naturally the big spending Departments and the Chief Executive's role becomes a particularly exacting one in times of central and local government financial constraint. In such times the heads of programme Departments are assailed by two forces. Council policy demands cuts in expenditure while each Department's staff demand that their Director fights to preserve the programme and services of the Department. It is the Chief Executive's responsibility to support the Departmental Director in resolving this conflict between Departments. He must give a wise lead to the Directors of Departments and understand their policies and difficulties.

279. The years since 1975 have been years of cuts in central and local government expenditure. The expectations of earlier years, in particular the DHSS 1972/3 growth projections for social services have become unrealisable. We consider that Mr Holt did not use his role as Chief Executive as wisely as he should have done in his dealings with Mr Douglas Jones and his Department. The main explanation for this was personal incompatibility and differing backgrounds. We feel that Mr Holt should have made more effort to make Mr Douglas Jones, the stranger in the authority, at home. The physical distance between the headquarters of Social Services in Birkenhead and the political and administrative power base in Wallasey increased the isolation of Mr Douglas Jones.

**The Triumvirate**

280. In the early years of the authority the Chief Executive and the eight Departmental Directors formed the Management Team of the authority. The Management Team met fortnightly and considered reports on major policy issues before these were submitted to programme Committees. This system

gradually came under attack from the opposition and the majority party on the Council and it was claimed that Chief Officers were spending too much of their time on general issues and not enough time on running their Departments. In November 1976 the Management Team was replaced by 'the Executive' which consisted of the Chief Executive, the Director of Administration and Legal Services and the Director of Finance. In the following year the management structure on the members' side was also reorganised and the Policy Group comprising the Committee Chairmen was formed.

281. The triumvirate, as it was publicly dubbed, was widely unpopular with the Directors of programme Departments. Its weakness was the uniformity of background of its membership: Mr Holt was a solicitor like Mr Mills (who became Director of Administration and Legal Services in December 1976, having been acting Director since May) and for most of the time the Leader of the Council was a chartered accountant. The strengths of the triumvirate were its professional expertise and its rapport with the Policy Group. This led staff of the Social Services Department to believe that matters directly involving their Department were being decided over the head of Mr Douglas Jones. There was indeed a lack of consultation and proper notification with Mr Douglas Jones before decisions were taken by Mr Holt (or the Executive) and the Chairman of the Social Services Committee. This led to mutual suspicion and recrimination between Mr Holt and Mr Douglas Jones.

282. By 1979 the Executive had like the Management Team before it fallen into disfavour. There were political criticisms about the power of the three members of the Executive and criticisms from other Directors about their own isolation. In June 1979 the Executive was replaced by the Chief Officers Group—effectively the old Management Team under a new name.

**Councillor Roberts**

283. From March 1976 until May 1978 Councillor Roberts was the Chairman of the Social Services Committee. He assumed a highly eccentric role. He was not merely interventionist, he interfered in the actual detailed running of the Department. He made excessive demands on senior management in the referral of individual cases. He was an aggressive personality given to dramatic and inappropriate phrases (such as 'heads will roll') when shortcomings occurred in the Department. Although he had the interests of the Department at heart his method of working was unpredictable. He would make policy decisions and policy changes without first considering the implications in depth with Mr Douglas Jones. He would cast hasty aspersions on Mr Douglas Jones and other members of staff. His style of chairmanship helped to undermine the effectiveness of the management and work of the Department.

**The role of the Councillor**

284. In general, we were impressed with the quality of the Councillors who gave evidence before us. In particular we found that those who came on to the Social Services Committee came from personal choice and inclination and a real interest in welfare. They understood their role, and it is important that it should be understood, to be that of policy makers having general

supervision of the Department. Their role was not to intervene in the professional handling of individual cases; casework must be left to the professional social worker.

285. Inevitably the conscientious Councillor will receive requests for help of a welfare nature. It is right that he should assess those requests and channel them in the right direction. However there can be and in our view there was in the case of Councillor Roberts such a volume of requests that a Social Services Department becomes unfairly burdened and pressurised. **We feel that Councillors should exercise a measure of restraint and should not expect referrals coming through them to receive priority as of right.**

**The letter of the 5th May 1978**

286. Mr Douglas Jones has always been keen to achieve as much as he could for his Department but he has not always been sensitive or subtle about trying to get what he wants. He attacks head on. After only a few months in office, when the effects of reorganisation were still being keenly felt he produced an 80-page Development Plan for Social Services. This plan was not viewed favourably by the Social Services Committee and the other Directors since it was not costed and it gave no details of the timing of the proposed improvements. Mr Douglas Jones was not good at receiving criticism or advice and tended to become aggressive when this happened, which had in the past made him rather unpopular with the other Directors. There was also the incompatibility between Mr Douglas Jones and Mr Holt and much more so between Mr Douglas Jones and Councillor Roberts. The Paul Brown tragedy produced responses from Councillor Roberts of 'Heads will roll' and 'Blood will flow' which isolated the Social Services Department more than ever. These feelings of reprisals and blame began to be felt throughout the Social Services Department and consequently morale suffered.

287. Two events in particular led to very severe criticism of Mr Douglas Jones by the Council which culminated on the 5th May 1978 in a letter being sent to Mr Douglas Jones which threatened dismissal if there was no improvement by the end of the year. These two events were the suggested closure of the Deeside Area Office as part of a savings exercise and the proposal to appoint an Assistant Director (Forward Planning and Development). By the end of 1977 both these recommendations of the Council had been virtually blocked by the Director, a situation which caused a great deal of friction over the years between the Director and the Council.

288. Against this background came a series of events in April 1978 that caused the situation to reach breaking point:

a. The Oakes report, discussed by the Council on the 10th April 1978, pointed out some of the failures of the Department in respect of Paul Brown.

b. An article appeared in the Birkenhead News on the 21st April which appeared to have the approval of Mr Douglas Jones, pointing out that because so few of his earlier recommendations had been fulfilled Wirral were lucky to have had only one Paul Brown tragedy.

c. In the same newspaper was a comment on a disagreement between Mr Douglas Jones and NALGO over an article some social workers had written for two social work publications highlighting their grievances and low morale. At 9am on the morning that he received the newspaper Councillor Roberts telephoned Wallasey Town Hall demanding Mr Douglas Jones' resignation.

d. The Deputy Area Officer at Central Wirral, Mrs Winship, spoke to her Councillor (Mrs Wood) and the Vice Chairman of the Social Services Committee (Councillor Ken Allen) on the 22nd April and complained about top management in Social Services, using words such as 'reprisals and repression from top management but no support or encouragement'. She felt too many resources were being put into community development and not enough into field social work. She also mentioned the Director's inability to accept criticism and the shortage of qualified social workers in Wirral. According to her, top management was hated at Central Wirral. (In evidence to us Mrs Winship told us that for the last two years most of the complaints were no longer valid and morale was improving fast).

e. Councillor Walker's assertion that a memo had been suppressed by the Social Services Department during the Oakes Inquiry and the implied suggestion that it had then been removed by them cast the Director in an even more unfavourable light.

289. These events led to a meeting of the Policy Group (ie the chairmen of Committees) on the 2nd May 1978 at which the Chief Executive, the Director of Administration and Legal Services, and the Director of Finance were asked to attend. This meeting was called to:

> 'consider the growing dissatisfaction at the way in which the Director of Social Services was failing to carry out efficiently the duties of his office'.

The minutes of the meeting include the following passage:

> 'Members expressed a lack confidence in the Director, and reference was made to his unwillingness to accept criticism or to take advice from others on the way in which his department should be more effectively organised. Notwithstanding a substantial increase in the resources made available for Social Services during a very difficult period of government restraint on public expenditure over the last two or three years, the Director constantly referred to a lack of resources and had been obstructive in the implementation of recommendations made following O and M reviews which had been instituted following a DHSS survey carried out in November 1976. Reference was also made to difficult staff relations within the department, to a lowering of morale, and the difficulty of recruiting qualified social workers and other staff because of the bad reputation which it was felt the Social Services Department in Wirral had been given primarily because of mishandling of departmental matters by the Director'.

The source of this paragraph was largely Mrs Winship's discussion with Councillor Mrs Wood. The evidence of Councillor Leigh (the current Chairman of the Social Services Committee), which we accept, was that the case against Mr Douglas Jones came largely from Councillor Roberts.

290. As a result of this meeting a letter was written by the Chief Executive to Mr Douglas Jones, on the instruction of the Policy Group. This letter, dated 5th May 1978, declared the dissatisfaction felt by the Policy Group and ended by saying:

> 'A period up to the end of this year is being allowed, during which the members will expect a substantial improvement in the discharge of your duties as Director, and the matter will be reviewed at that time. If there is no such improvement or there is any other serious failure adequately to discharge your duties during the intervening period, I must warn you that your continued employment with this authority will not be countenanced'.

After many requests by Mr Douglas Jones to be allowed to state his point of view, he was received in audience before the Policy Group in April 1979. A further letter was then sent saying that no action would be taken regarding Mr Douglas Jones' continued employment but that he must carry out the Council's decisions in particular in respect of the closure of the Deeside Office and the appointment of the Assistant Director (Forward Planning).

291. In February 1978 Mr SeQueira was appointed as Deputy director and in May 1978 Councillor Leigh took over as Chairman of the Social Services Committee from Councillor Roberts. The careful guidance of Councillor Leigh and the support of Mr SeQueira have enabled Mr Jones to achieve a great deal. In our visits to the various parts of the Social Services Department we have noted the relaxed relationship between the staff and Mr Douglas Jones which has given us considerable hope for the future.

292. Two days before the end of our Inquiry, Counsel for the Wirral Borough Council made the following statement:

> 'On the Saturday morning two weeks ago that we sat to hear evidence you, Sir, asked me whether the letter of 5 May was now dead and gone. I said that I believed so but that Mr Holt might be better able to deal with that matter. Mr Holt gave you a rather qualified answer to that because it depended to a great extent upon his political masters.
>
> I am now able to say that those political masters have instructed me to make a statement about that and it is in these terms: that the letter of 5 May 1978 will not be referred to again and can now be treated as having gone. So far as the Council is concerned, it is a matter which is over. It is a closed book.
>
> That of course does not mean that the Director of Social Services is to have carte blanche to behave in the way that he wishes; it puts him in the same position as everybody else, but at least in my submission it clears the decks for the future. It is not a matter of taking it out of the file and destroying it; it is public knowledge now, but the Council takes the view that it is a matter upon which it no longer wishes to rely and it, as is I hope everybody else, is looking to the future and the morale of the department.'

**Conclusion**

293. The effectiveness of the Wirral Social Services Department will, in the years ahead, depend to a very large extent on the attitudes and morale of the staff who have lived through the Paul Brown tragedy. Many changes in child care practice have been made in the Social Services Department since the report of the Oakes Inquiry in 1978 and we were impressed by the good work being done in the offices which we visited and the calibre of the staff who are working in the Department. Mr Douglas Jones has many qualities which could contribute to providing Wirral with an excellent Social Services Department and he deserves support from Council Members and from other Departments, as well as from the general public. **At the end of our Inquiry Mr Holt and others offered Mr Douglas Jones an olive branch, an offer to start afresh once the Inquiry was over, and create a more productive working relationship. If Mr Douglas Jones is willing to reciprocate with an improved appreciation of the problems of his colleagues and in particular of the need to live with economic and political constraints we believe that Wirral can face the future with confidence.**

294. Under the wise leadership of the present Chairman, Councillor Leigh, we are satisfied that the Social Services Committee can fulfil its role and give positive support and advice to Mr Douglas Jones. **With mutual support there is no reason why Committee and Department should not function well.**

## REPRESENTATION OF PARTIES

| *Representatives* | *Parties* |
|---|---|
| Mr Simon Fawcus and Mr Keith Armitage instructed by the Treasury Solicitor | The Committee |
| Mr David Aubrey instructed by Messrs Haworth and Gallagher | Mr A Pickstock |
| Miss Cherie Booth instructed by Messrs Hodge, Jones and Allen | Mrs Pauline Brown |
| Mr M H Byrde | Miss A M Lloyd |
| Mr Maxwell Cooke | Mrs Anders |
| Mr R Hamilton instructed by Mr A Gibbons, Solicitor and Legal Adviser to Mersey Regional Health Authority | Wirral Area Health Authority |
| Mr John Hedgecoe | Mr P N Samuels |
| Mr Mark Hedley instructed by Bremner Sons and Corlett | Mrs Doran |
| Miss Lyndsey Kushner | Mrs Sayer |
| Mr David Lynch instructed by Messrs Morecrofts and Owen Dawson | National and Local Government Officers Association |
| Mr Andrew Main and Mr John Trotter | British Association of Social Workers |
| Mr John Morgan instructed by Mr P J Mills of Wirral Borough Council | Wirral Borough Council |
| Miss Heather Steel instructed by Mr Wilson of Merseyside County Council | Chief Constable of Merseyside and the Merseyside Probation and After Care Service |
| Mr Jon Williams instructed by Messrs Hempsons | Doctors |

Printed for Her Majesty's Stationery Office by Bemrose Specialist Print, Derby
Dd 294646 K28 12/80